Remembrance

CRUSE BEREAVEMENT CARE

Founded in 1959, Cruse Bereavement Care is a national charity offering help to all who are bereaved.

The death of someone close can affect us in several different ways – emotionally, physically, socially and in many practical areas of our life. Cruse offers free personal and confidential help, giving counselling, across the UK and a bereavement support service and helpline from our central office in Richmond.

Memorial services play a valuable part in the healing process of grief and this anthology is a fitting tribute to the lives remembered here that have enriched us all, to those who have been bereaved and to those who have given freely of their time to share words and music that hold a particular significance for them.

Remembrance

An Anthology of Readings, Prayers and Music
chosen for Memorial Services

INTRODUCED BY

NED SHERRIN

FOREWORD BY

THE ARCHBISHOP OF CANTERBURY

MICHAEL JOSEPH

LONDON

MICHAEL JOSEPH LTD

Published by the Penguin Group
27 Wrights Lane, London w8 5TZ
Viking Penguin Inc., 375 Hudson Street, New York, New York 10014, USA
Penguin Books Australia Ltd, Ringwood, Victoria, Australia
Penguin Books Canada Ltd, 10 Alcorn Avenue, Toronto, Ontario, Canada M4V 3B2
Penguin Books (NZ) Ltd, 182–190 Wairau Road, Auckland 10, New Zealand

Penguin Books Ltd, Registered Offices: Harmondsworth, Middlesex, England

First published in Great Britain 1996
This anthology copyright © Michael Joseph 1996
Introduction copyright © Ned Sherrin 1996
Copyright individual services and contributions, and individual poems, prayers, readings
and songs, as in the Acknowledgements page 269
1 3 5 7 9 10 8 6 4 2

Set in 11/12½pt Monophoto Bembo
Typeset by Datix International Limited, Bungay, Suffolk
Printed in England by Clays Ltd, St Ives plc

A CIP catalogue record for this book is available from the British Library

ISBN 0 7181 3871 6

All royalties from this book are to be donated to:

Cruse House, 126 Sheen Road, Richmond, Surrey TW9 1UR
Tel: 0181 940 4818   Fax: 0181 940 7638
Cruse Bereavement Line: 0181 332 7227

Registered Charity No. 208078

CONTENTS

FOREWORD

Saying a proper 'farewell' is, as many studies have shown, a vital part of the bereavement process. Funeral services have an important role to play in this, as, in many cases, do memorial ones. I am delighted, therefore, as a patron of Cruse Bereavement Care, that this anthology has now been published. Memorial services need both to be personal and to form a fitting tribute to the one who has died. They therefore need words, music and prayers that say the right things in that particular context. Finding these can be a very difficult task indeed and I am sure that *Remembrance* will prove to be a very useful sourcebook for people setting out to plan such a service. I hope, therefore, that it will be used widely in the years ahead.

+ George Cantuar

Archbishop of Canterbury

INTRODUCTION

Back in 1992 I received a letter from Richard Ingrams, the editor of *The Oldie* magazine. 'Dear Ned,' he wrote, 'Would you like to review memorial services for us? I am told that you go to nearly all of them.' Richard got his piece of not-quite-accurate information from Keith Waterhouse and Victoria Mather; but it is true that I have made a habit of attending the memorial services of friends over the years. And felt better for it.

A memorial service is not only a chance to pay respects and to celebrate a person's life. It is often a happy way to put a period to a time of mourning. Funerals arrive too soon. Even so, after arranging for my collaborator Caryl Brahms' memorial service at St Paul's, Covent Garden, I had a recurring dream in which she would turn up to press a point and I would explain how inconvenient this was as there has been a full house for her send-off and how surprised everyone would be at her re-appearance. Gradually the dream faded and it no longer comes to me: but there was something comforting in arranging the service. In Caryl's case it was largely a selection of readings and songs from her own work – and a violin/piano duet by two very young protégés of hers who have gone on to fine careers as professional musicians a dozen or so years later. Dorothy Tutin, one of Caryl's favourite great actresses, did a bravura reading from *No Bed for Bacon* and David Kernan sang the last song she wrote (with Mark Wilkinson) beautifully.

I was happy to record services for *The Oldie* as I had so many rich memories of moving moments on earlier occasions. Barbara Windsor singing 'The Boy I Love is up in the Gallery' for Kenneth Williams. Evelyn Laye gaily conjuring up John Gilpin from the pulpit at St Martin's in the Fields. Dame Sybil Thorndike's service in Westminster Abbey: Sybil loved trumpets and tremendous clarion calls blew her over to the other side. At Donald Wolfit's service in St Martin's in the Fields, Paul Scofield was an usher and I followed a little woman, plainly a Wolfit fan, bent double with age, as he showed her to her pew. When she was settled he gave her the order of service. She unbent to look up and thank him. Immediately she recognized him. 'Oh,' she gasped, 'you're Paul Scofield.' 'Yes,' Paul replied gently, 'but we're not here for that, are we?'

Americans often have a more secular approach to remembrance – friends and relations will perhaps gather in a room to share their memories. Sometimes a theatre is taken and the stage is filled with the theatrical great and good who bear testimony. When the leading American theatrical lawyer Arnold Weissburger died, his devoted companion, Milton Goldman, assembled at the Golden Theatre a cast which included Louise Rainer, Orson Welles and Martha Graham. Arnold's signature white carnation and silk evening scarf occupied a prominent position on the side of the stage. Then with suitable changes of cast Milton 'toured' the ceremony to Los Angeles and to the Haymarket Theatre in London, where he in turn was remembered in the fullness of time.

This admirable (and useful) book will be an invaluable source for those who have to plan a memorial service. Most of the perennial favourites are here; and some rewarding surprises. But I missed Noël Coward's

> When I have fears, as Keats had fears,
> Of the moment I'll cease to be
> I console myself with vanished years
> Remembered laughter, remembered tears,
> And the peace of the changing sea.
>
> When I feel sad, as Keats felt sad
> That my life is so nearly done
> It gives me comfort to dwell upon
> Remembered friends who are dead and gone
> And the jokes we had and the fun.
>
> How happy they are I cannot know,
> But happy am I who loved them so.

And If you want to strike a lighter note this one – also by Coward – might do the trick:

> I'm here for a short visit only,
> And I'd rather be loved than hated.
> Eternity may be lonely
> When my body's disintegrated;
> And that which is loosely termed my soul
> Goes whizzing off through the infinite
> By means of some vague remote control.
> I'd like to think I was missed a bit.

Canon Henry Scott Holland's 'Death is nothing at all . . .' (page 67) is probably the most quoted reading – along with 'We would ask now of death . . .' from *The Prophet* Kahlil Gibran, (page 73). One of my own favourites is Plato's *The Last Days of Socrates* (on page 81) which I first heard when Bernard Levin chose it for that considerable actress, Yvonne Mitchell's, funeral.

What of new memorial *Top of the Pops*? W. H. Auden's poem 'Funeral Blues' – quoted by John Hannah in the film *Four Weddings and a Funeral* after the death of Simon Callow's character – is already climbing the charts. But I have a dark horse tip. It is not published until autumn 1996, when it appears in *Armada*, a collection of poems and elegies by Brian Patten. He read it on *Loose Ends* on BBC Radio 4 and we received an unprecedented number of requests for copies. The saddest came to me from a recently widowed woman who wanted to read it at her husband's funeral, but the letter got to me too late, after post-room delays. The poem speaks with such a universal voice that I am sure it will strike a chord.

HOW LONG IS A MAN'S LIFE?

Cuanto vive el hombre por fin? Vive mil dias o uno solo?
Una Semana o varios siglos? Por cuanto tiempo muere el hombre?
Que quiere decir 'para siempre'? – Pablo Neruda

How long does a man live, after all?
A thousand days, or only one?
One week, or a few centuries?
How long does a man spend living or dying
and what do we mean when we say, gone forever?

Adrift in such preoccupations, we seek clarification.
We can go to the philosophers,
but they will weary of our questions.
We can go to the priests and the rabbis
but they might be too busy with administrations.

So, How long does a man live, after all?
And how much does he live while he lives?
We fret, and ask so many questions –
then when it comes to us
the answer is so simple after all.

A man lives for as long as we carry him inside us,
for as long as we carry the harvest of his dreams,
for as long as we ourselves live,
holding memories in common, a man lives.

His lover will carry his man's scent, his touch;
his children will carry the weight of his love.
One friend will carry his arguments,
another will hum his favourite tunes,
another will still share his terrors.

And the days will pass with baffled faces,
then the weeks, then the months,
then there will be a day when no question is asked,
and the knots of grief will loosen in the stomach,
and the puffed faces will calm.
And on that day he will not have ceased,
     but will have ceased to be separated by death.
How long does a man live, after all?

A man lives so many different lengths of time.

Quite a few of the orders of service included at the back of this book record memorials I have attended. The printed order of service for Julian Belfrage, theatrical agent, cannot reveal the emotion bravely controlled by Julian's client, Judi Dench, reading the Henry Scott Holland piece; or the revision wrought by Dan Day Lewis who, instead of reading the advertised 'Lights Out' by Edward Thomas, told a wild and wonderful story of a train trip to York with Julian and then sang *acapella* a lovely lament; or the two sons Robin and Crispin reading 'Lord Hippo' by Belloc and Pearman's 'Londonderry Air'; or Ronan Browne from Ireland playing 'Old Bush' and 'Braes of Busby'; or the heady mixture of Stage and Turf which filled the church; and the choir who raised the roof with 'Sit Down You're Rocking the Boat'.

Readers may find it interesting to see the effect Sir Kenneth MacMillan's memorial service had on your reviewer.

In some magical way Westminster Abbey took on the intimacy of a parish church on Wednesday, 17 February 1993.

Deborah and Charlotte, Kenneth MacMillan's widow and daughter, were surrounded by devoted friends and balletomanes, and the nave was filled with his extended family – awed children's faces from the Royal Ballet School alongside colleagues from the Company.

The Abbey, which can do these things with such pomp, found a simple splendour for the man who inspired the heartfelt thanksgiving – and who died at only sixty-three.

Does Dame Ninette de Valois OM CM DBE (ninety-four) wonder how many more celebrations of the lives of her protégés she must attend? She found words for Anthony Dowell CBE to speak on her behalf which placed MacMillan properly and pre-eminently on the world stage.

Big black hats, stoved and brimmed, were out in force. Lady Bonham Carter, Ginesta Mackintosh and Lady Soames (who slipped me one of the cough sweets she hands out to her audiences at the National Theatre, to stop a fit of barking) wore the biggest. Lynn Seymour CBE had the sauciest – she read a powerful metaphor for taming the spirit of the dance, C. Day Lewis's 'Pegasus'. Lady Harlech's jet mane is a hat in its own right.

Two addresses were given: one by Peter Wright CBE, director of Birmingham Royal Ballet, who knew MacMillan throughout both their careers, and the other by Nicholas Hytner who directed his last new work, the dances for *Carousel* at the National Theatre. Those who arrived later than the 11.30 time, suggested on the invitation, missed an inspired performance of the Carousel Waltz, conducted by Barry Wordsworth.

Hytner had been nervous, he said, when he approached the great man and had rattled on, finally blurting out, 'The point is it's all about sex and violence', at which Kenneth had smiled and said, 'That's what I do!'

The last dance MacMillan made was for the exuberant 'June is Bustin' Out All Over'. He was unmoved by the fulsome excitement the first run-through generated, until the dialect coach said, 'It's like an orgy on *speed*.' He spent the rest of the day happily repeating the phrase.

Unspeedily, in stark simplicity, little Simon de Baat, a chorister, sent us home with Faure's 'Pie Jesu' from his *Requiem*, accompanied by the Royal Sinfonia. It was conducted by the Abbey's Martin Neary, as was all the choral singing.

Of services not included in this book, here is a sampling of my reviews of the most memorable. The first time I went as a reviewer was at the service for Dame Gwen Ffrangcon-Davies (1891–1992) on 18 June 1992.

It is hard to beat a theatrical memorial service. The flower of Equity is on parade and with a subject as loved, revered and, not to put too fine a point on it, as *old* as Dame Gwen was, there was much to comfort and uplift at the Royal Parish Church of St Martin's in the Fields.

When Dame Gwen heard that the life of her great friend Dame Edith Evans

(1888–1976) was to be celebrated at St Paul's, she is famously reported to have said, 'She'll never fill it!' However, the St Paul's in question was the one in Covent Garden, and Dame Edith's loyal peers and public filled that church just as Dame Gwen's did at St Martin's on 18 June.

The 'Thanksgiving for the Life' of Dame Gwen fell somewhere between the very grand and the intimate. Paul Scofield kicked off with St John I: 1–14: 'In the beginning was the word . . .', his resonant brown voice softened to accommodate the microphone. Anna Massey read Christina Rossetti's 'Remember', and Hilary Jenkyns stood well back to sing 'The Faery Song' from Rutland Boughton's *The Immortal Hour*. 'Gwenny used to sing that,' clucked one old dear in front of me approvingly.

Yes, she first sang it at the Glastonbury Festival seventy-three years ago. It's the one which starts: 'How beautiful they are, the Lordly Ones . . .', and ends up, unfortunately, with Noël Coward's verdict on ENSA: 'They laugh and are glad and are terrible.'

Dame Wendy Hiller (1912–) made her frail way to the dais to speak one of Elizabeth Barrett Browning's *Sonnets from the Portuguese*, 'I shall but love thee better after death'. George Baker forsook his Inspector Wexford accent for Kipling's 'The Glory of the Garden'. 'I've never heard that before,' muttered another old biddy behind me. At her age, she should have.

There were two recordings of Dame Gwen's incredibly youthful voice and a reading from her witty diary by Dorothy Tutin, who has the same trick of sounding seventeen and will still have it when *she* is 101.

John Gielgud's first Romeo was played opposite a patient Gwen Ffrangcon-Davies. He was twenty and she an experienced thirty-four. He spoke Romeo's last lines from Peggy Ashcroft's signed copy. Sir John (1904–) is usually asked for 'Fear no more the heat of the sun' on these occasions. His voice no longer aspires to youth but all the intelligence and beauty were there. For once the famous Terry tears were on hold.

Nigel Hawthorne's address alternated between overpowering emotion and marvellous memories. Interviewing Gwen for television he had asked her if she was afraid of death. With her peculiar, gay, high-seriousness she replied, 'I'm always nervous of doing something for the first time.'

At another friend's graveside the vicar had invited her to cast the first dust on to the coffin. 'Not down, you silly old fool,' she had snapped, 'Up!' 'Quite right,' the vicar of St Martin's added in his prayer.

The Stambourne Singers from the village where she lived for fifty years then sent her aloft with a charming warning to her new colleagues: 'Hark all ye lovely saints'.

I would estimate that the fine actor Robert Harris (1900–) was the most senior of the congregation.

Sadly Robert Harris died last year.

A month later there was a very different service at St Margaret's, Westminster, on Wednesday 22 July.

ARTHUR FRANCIS BENJAMIN GUINNESS
EARL OF IVEAGH 1937–1992

I had never before been to a service of thanksgiving for the life of a person I did not know. However, reassured by the announcement, 'Tickets are not required. All are welcome', your critic took his place with the great and the good.

Princess Alexandra was represented; so were two ambassadors. Three foreign-sounding princes and princesses were there, two homegrown dukes and duchesses, a marchioness, a handful of earls, countesses, viscounts and their ladies, a battery of barons and theirs; a mixture of peerage and beerage, Mr Auberon and Lady Teresa Waugh.

The piquancy of the occasion lay in the recently troubled history of the Guinness empire, into whose service Arthur Guinness, Earl of Iveagh, beckoned Ernest Saunders, and from whose offices he banished him after Saunders had made a great deal of money for the Guinness family and their shareholders in questionable circumstances.

Viscountess Blakenham had the difficult task of eulogizing an old friend whose modest life ended in illness and professional disarray. He outlined Iveagh's early years; his father's tragic death at Arnhem when Arthur was six, pitchforking him into direct succession to his grandfather; his journey (aged ten) to give away his mother on the occasion of her happy, second marriage; his popularity at Eton; his assumption of command at twenty-six; his shyness; his remarkable collection of Irish first editions.

Eventually, Blakenham grasped the nettle and earned a place in the *Guinness Book of Tactful Tightrope-Walking*. Pausing a moment, he volunteered: 'Meanwhile, a number of things had begun to go wrong . . . the introduction of professional management,' he said (making a bid for the *Guinness Book of Understatement*), 'had far-reaching consequences . . . not all of them good.'

Moving away from controversy, he speculated that his friend was more appreciated in Ireland than here. The service reflected his Anglo–Irish allegiances.

The new Earl of Iveagh read from the Wisdom of Solomon: 'All those things are passed away like a shadow . . .' His brother Rory read from St John: 'In my father's house are many mansions . . .' The anthem was Spenser's 'Faire is the heav'n', set by William H. Harris. There were prayers from three Irish prayer books. The choir sang verses from *St Patrick's Breastplate* and we chorused an eighth-century Irish hymn, 'High King of Heaven, thou heaven's bright Sun,/O grant me its joys after vict'ry is won.'

We were left to ponder Lord Blakenham's final words, 'A gentle, good and lovely man; and that is how we will remember him.' I did not see the erstwhile Alzheimer's sufferer, Ernest Saunders. Perhaps he forgot.

In October of the same year I was back in the same church for a journalist friend.

PETER JENKINS 1934–1992
St Margaret's Church, Westminster Abbey

On 19 October, appropriately hours before one of the more dramatic political somersaults of recent years, a full house of the Great and Would-be-Good celebrated the life of Peter Jenkins, political pundit of the *Independent*. Michael Heseltine, the acrobat without the net, read from John Donne's *Devotions on Emergent Occasions*. Before, he said he realized that Peter would have enjoyed the 'exquisite irony' in the words he was about to speak, 'Never send to know for whom the bell tolls, it tolls for thee.'

That brought a wintry smile from Neil Kinnock, who had chosen a pew near the back, just in front of me, along with other Labour frontbenchers past and present, including Tony Blair and Mo Mowlam. Mr Kinnock's fine Welsh voice rang out particularly in 'Guide me, O thou great redeemer' to the tune of Cwm Rhondda, the words of which he knew by heart.

Grandees such as John Smith, Lord (Cecil) Parkinson and Lord (Roy) Jenkins gravitated importantly to the front, along with the American ambassador.

The warmth of affection for Jenkins was clear from the introductions of the three readers. Liz Forgan of Channel 4 was standing in for Lord Owen ('unavoidably absent'). Before I. Corinthians, 15 she recalled a Washington encounter with the shattered correspondent who was calling loudly for champagne to wash away a week spent in South Dakota observing the hype on the Reagan campaign plane.

Heseltine admitted that he could have used Peter's advice during his traumatic preceding few days; and Julian Mitchell gave a vivid account of his friend's varied enthusiasms – politics, journalism, food, drink, painting, farming, playwriting, gardening, music and housebuilding in Italy. Even his depressions, he said, were played to the hilt. 'Peter was the only man I have ever met who, even when depressed, was depressed with gusto.' Then he read Dylan Thomas's 'Do Not Go Gentle'.

Poor Andreas Whittam-Smith, Jenkins' last editor, will never set the chancel on a roar, so after some moving readers' letters he wisely stuck to his subject's courage and his outstanding professional achievements. Those whose eyes strayed to read Ronald Dworkin's more lively and personal address (at the funeral) reprinted at the back of the order of service, could be forgiven.

The order itself gave an affectionate nod to Peter Jenkins' previous employer *The Grauniad* with at least two misprints. My favourite was 'No man is an inland.'

The choir of St Margaret's was on top form with Fauré's 'Pie Jesu', the Easter Hymn from *Cavalleria Rusticana* and Orlando Gibbons' 'Threefold Amen'.

On the way out a nice Irish woman remarked on emerging what a beautiful service it had been – 'if a bit on the serious side'.

The theatrical profession was out in force at St Pauls, Covent Garden, on 28 January 1993.

JOE MITCHENSON 1911–1992

Fortnum and Mason, Swan and Edgar, Mander and Mitchenson . . . the two theatre archivists were inseparable until Raymond Mander died nine years ago. Many confused them. Raymond looked like a Joe and Joe looked like a Raymond. Noël Coward called them 'Gog and Magog' – and left each a dressing gown in his will. Mary Clare christened them 'the boys'. Sybil Thorndike spoke for the profession when she said, 'The boys are our passport to posterity.'

At St Paul's Judi Dench remembered them as 'fairy godfathers' who would by now be 'organizing heaven'. Mary Miller read an inspired choice from Don Marquis: Tom, the old trouper cat, who was kicked by Mansfield, played a bloodhound in *Uncle Tom's Cabin* and had an ancestor who dropped from the flies to play Jefferson's beard when the stuck-on piece fell off – unlike modern cats, 'he had stage presence . . . he had it *here*.'

Timothy West's passages from the actor-manager John Coleman were just as fresh, ranging from a *Tempest* in Glasgow in 1851 when Ariel's rope snapped and she broke both legs ('I was playing in Cardiff on the Monday so never knew what happened to her') to 1890 when he was touring seventy works ('One rehearsal for some – many with none').

The music matched the man. Lorna Dallas sang late and vintage Coward. The Players' Theatre choir ended appropriately with Novello's 'Glamorous Night'. Inveterate first-nighters, M. and M. assembled an unrivalled theatre collection at Venner Road where Joe lived for sixty years. Now it is in Beckenham.

Felix Barker's warm address hinted that the jeopardy in which it stands may be nearly over. That would be the best thanksgiving for a unique partnership.

In April of that year Barbara Kelly-Braden organized the service for her husband.

BERNARD CHASTEY BRADEN 1916–1993

The affectionate farewell to Bernard Braden at St Paul's, Covent Garden, was the jolliest I can remember. The Revd Roger Royle's *Bidding* ('What is he starting at?' inquired a racing man, Sir Clement Freud) set up Braden's debt to his parson father, his humour and the problems of beginning as an actor in Canada. People said, 'If he was any good he'd have emigrated to the United States or England'; then there was his early BBC Radio and TV shows, including 'the Corporation's Director of the Unspoken Word – in charge of pauses, commas and coughs'.

From his diary, Bernard's son Christopher raised a lot of laughs.

A Bouquet for Bernie was offered by James Burke, Barry Cryer and Peter Cook – who confessed to your critic that he had never been to a memorial service before. He may become an addict. He resurrected E. L. Wisty, the character Braden invited him to recreate for TV when he returned from a two-year triumph on Broadway thinking he was famous here and found he was not. It was good to hear of the World Domination Party again, even though it was meant to take over in 1967. Barry Cryer's tribute was in verse with more puns per line than is decent. James Burke recalled a luxurious afternoon with the overstretched Bradens on the Riviera with Bernie insisting in his 'Gabby' voice, 'First class! It's the only way to go!'

There was music from Anita Harris and Kenny Clayton. Brian Tesler evoked Braden the innovator. His was the first *weekly* TV comedy series. Until then the BBC thought it impossible for actors to learn their lines in less than two weeks. Bernie overcame that by introducing the new-fangled American 'tele-prompter' of which he became the first master.

Bernard Levin's more philosophical piece remarked that Braden shared his birth date with Liberace and with the coronation of Napoleon. He praised his unexpected humour: 'Whenever I meet a pretty girl it turns out she's married – or I am!' And he insisted that Braden's hobby in *Who's Who*, 'finding time', meant finding time for others.

Kim Braden spoke of her father's humorous legacy spanning the generations – and the continents – through her son and his American schoolfellows. She read the cemetery poem from *The Spoon River Anthology*.

Bernard Braden's own recording of Chesterton's 'The Donkey' ended a service sprinkled with laughter and warm applause which broke out again as the widow Braden and her brood left St Paul's proudly through their friends.

ADELAIDE HALL (1901–1993)
St Paul's, Covent Garden

FREDERICK EDWARD NEUFLIZE PONSONBY
10TH EARL OF BESSBOROUGH DL (1913–1993)
St Margaret's Westminster

Connoisseurs of memorial services could hardly have looked for greater contrast in thanksgivings than those which recently celebrated the lives of two splendid survivors – both with theatrical connections.

Adelaide Hall's whole life was music and theatre. So was her send-off, which drew friends, fans and musical theatre veterans.

Eric Bessborough was, among other valuable things, a devoted *aficionado* of the theatre. His service beckoned, at a rough count, a Bishop, a Duchess, eight Viscounts, a suitable consort of Viscountesses, eight Earls, many Countesses, half a dozen Baronesses, thirty-eight Lords, nearly as many, perhaps more, Ladies, Black Rod, six MPs and again, a lot of friends.

The Earl and the Girl would have loved each other's celebrations. Adelaide would have relished the stately pace of Eric's service. She might have chucked Lord Hailsham (a much younger man) under the chin on his way out and told him how well he read Wisdom 5: 9–16, 'All those things are passed away like a shadow.' She would certainly have tapped Patrick Garland on the shoulder as he followed, having realized, when he beautifully read Belloc's 'Duncton Hill' (in recognition of Eric's passion for Sussex), that Patrick ran the Chichester Theatre and there might be a gig for her at the Minerva.

Eric – he had been at St Paul's – would have delighted in Adelaide's foot-stomping order of service which started with 'Drop Me Off in Harlem.'

Immediately he would have recognized a special talent in Melanie Marshall who did 'Come Sunday' ample justice. He and Mary would have clapped along with the whole church when Beryl Bryden, referring to Joshua and Jericho, nearly brought the walls of the 'best barn in Europe' a-tumb-a-lin down.

Larry Adler's echo of Adelaide's 'Creole Love Call' improvisations to Ellington's theme would have had Eric as spellbound as it did the congregation. Michael Parkinson's funny and affectionate address would have made him smile and he might have cared to pass on the odd felicitious phrase to Anthony Nelson MP who delivered his own encomium.

There were no recordings of Eric to play at St Margaret's. Not even his fine, long-ago amateur Hamlet. But he would have marvelled at Adelaide's recording (at her ninetieth birthday) of 'I Can't Give You Anything but Love, Baby,' played as we left St Paul's.

Two generous souls would have enjoyed each other's obsequies. If they are now to meet they will enjoy each other – in spite of the twelve-year age difference.

On 16 May 1994 one of Britain's most popular broadcasters had one of the Abbey's most affectionate farewells. There had been some concern after the high jinks at Les Dawson's memorial that stricter control might be exercised. Anyway, Abbey and heirs contributed to a memorable occasion.

BRIAN JOHNSTON, CBE, MC (1912–1994)
Westminster Abbey

An Abbey memorial service which begins with 'The Eton Boating Song' and plays you out with 'Underneath the Arches' starts and finishes strongly. The Abbey stage managers never let down those it celebrates. You can rely on heart-stopping moments which upstage the rhetoric, the singing and the setting – but never pre-guess the effect. Sybil Thorndike had those trumpets to blow her away to the other side. With Laurence Olivier it was the parade of great actors bearing his emblems and awards. For Kenneth MacMillan it was a child fluting the 'Pie Jesu' from aloft.

For Johnners it was the Grenadiers. Two young Guards musicians playing the 'Grenadiers' Return' slow-marched the length of the nave, the quire and the sacrarium drumming and piping the tune in honour of a Guards MC. The drummer cannot have been born when Brian turned sixty.

Brother Christopher read Psalm 15: 'Lord, who shall dwell in Thy tabernacle?' Son Barry read his godfather Williams Douglas Home's 'A Glorious Game, Say We': 'Yes, cricket will live till the trumpet trumps/From the wide, pavilioned sky,/And time, the umpire lays low the stumps/As his scythe goes sweeping by . . .'

Colin Cowdrey and John Major gave addresses from parallel pulpits. Cowdrey represented the cricketing profession with the eloquence and humour of those memorable amateurs. The Prime Minister well conveyed the affection in which the ordinary man held Johnners.

After Michael Denison had done justice to Cardus on the outbreak of war seen from the Long Room, Richard Stilgoe, our leading occasional versifier, alluded to 'the bowler's holding . . .' without offending Dean, Chapter or Archbishop Runcie, and trumpeted two corking couplets. Of Brian's arrival in Heaven: 'He talks to total strangers,/Calls the Angel Gabriel "Angers"'; and of his new role as a heavenly greeter: 'When St Peter's done the honours,/ He will pass you on to Johnners'. You will recognize the seraph by his 'ears like wings and correspondent shoes' and the proferred 'angel-cake'.

The Prime Minister had not been perfectly briefed. The moving poem 'From a Blind Listener' was not, as he heralded it, 'by a little boy' (charming image) but by the mature Melvin Collins who read it strongly: 'Here was a friend to those who never knew him,/ Eyes to those who cannot see . . .'

For the last service I could hardly find a man more warmly remembered.

MERVYN STOCKWOOD
Cathedral of St Saviour & St Mary Overie,
Southwark 8 March 1995

I nearly missed this memorial because of the new fashionable time of three o'clock. I like the good old noon-and-on-to-lunch-and-reminiscence. As Arthur Marshall one said, 'Nothing sharpens the appetite for lunch like a good funeral.'

Bishop Mervyn's service was distinguished by a remarkable sermon by Lord Runcie. There had been scant warning of the occasion and I only knew about it because Robert Runcie had written to ask me if I knew any Mervyn jokes. Sadly, none he could use. I'd arrived without ticket and was cast into the outer darkness by a grim woman in a black headband who said sternly, 'You'll have to sit in the black seats.' I found a marginally more convenient spot among some anoraked priests on grey seats also at the back.

The service was beautifully sung and spoken; but its feature was Arch-bishop Runcie's wonderfully warm evocation of Mervyn, taking his text from

Ecclesiastes ('Cast your bread upon the waters . . .'). Ecclesiastes, he defined as 'the most mysterious and cynical book in the Bible'. He summoned up Mervyn's generosity, his conviviality, his politics and his spirituality in a variety of well-crafted phrases – Mervyn's and the scriptures. 'The heart of a wise man inclines to the right, the heart of a fool to the left . . .' Quoting Mervyn arriving at the University Church: 'Show me where to kiss the Remnants or are they already sitting in their pews?' His boredom with 'working parties' – 'paralysis by analysis'. 'A socialist who also loved the upper reaches of the social scale.' He mocked the traditional value judgement after death – 'He was all of a piece'. Mervyn, he insisted, was a generous mixture of men. 'Is it a bad thing to be more than one man?'

Finally he could not resist the ultimate Stockwood anecdote. At the last Lambeth conference Mervyn was on the list of bishops outed by Tatchell's Thought Police. The Bishop of Bath and Wells rang to warn him. Mervyn cut him short, 'Jim,' he said, 'I couldn't care tuppence. And if the Press get on to you, tell them I've had a lot of women too!'

In a rather snide article in the *Sunday Times* in June 1995 Christopher Middleton wrote, 'Forget world premières and charity galas. The place for celebrities to see and be seen these days is the memorial service. Not so much a first night as a positively last London performance . . . might there not be a market for a weekly televised memorial service – *This was Your Life* – with guest appearances from some of the biggest names in show-biz bereavement? Drama, music, glamour, tears – you've got to hand it to death; it's got the lot.'

The late Robert Morley refused to authorize a memorial service for himself and devoted some 2,000 words in *Punch* to knocking the idea. He likened these ceremonies to cocktail parties for geriatrics and wrote that nothing depressed him more than the sight of an actor in a pulpit.

I should like my own memorial service (if awarded) to come as a complete surprise. I should enjoy speculating on the contents. One request: perhaps Maria Friedman might be persuaded to sing a song Gerard Kenny and I wrote for her, 'A Funny Thing to be Alone, Not Funny.' And maybe someone might offer Rodgers and Hart's ballad, excluded from *Pal Joey*, 'I'm Talking to my Friend.' The rest, jolly!

Until that day I shall continue to attend the memorials of others and repeat Coward's words to myself:

> It gives me comfort to dwell upon
> Remembered friends who are dead and gone
> And the jokes we had and the fun.

NED SHERRIN
London
January, 1996

NOTE

A number of people were invited to contribute to this book, either by suggesting a programme for their own memorial service, or by giving permission to include a memorial service already held for someone else. The content of this book is based on the varied donations received. The publishers and Cruse, the charity that works for bereavement care, which will be receiving the royalties for this book, would like to express their sincere thanks to all those who so kindly contributed.

In the anthology, all Bible readings are given in the versions specified in the services. If several people chose the same thing (for example, broadly the same passage from the Bible but from different versions and omitting or including different verses), only one version, and the fullest, has been given. Only general prayers, in no particular order, have been included; the full text of bidding prayers and prayers for individuals, and of addresses, is not included.

Readings, poems, hymns and sung music are listed in order of popularity (hence, for example, 'Death is nothing at all', from Henry Scott Holland's sermon 'The King of Terrors', which appears first in the 'Readings' section, is the most popular choice of non-biblical reading in the contributions) and alphabetically if chosen by an equal number of people. 'Other Music' has been listed alphabetically by composer, with further information where available.

In the 'Hymns' section, authors and tunes have been given where available. In the 'Sung Music' section, where possible an English translation has been provided, in italics, following the original. If known, the authors of the lyrics follow the names of the composers.

In some cases it has not been possible to trace or obtain permission to include the full texts.

The section 'The Contributors', beginning on page 213, summarizes the services, listing in order the titles of the works included in each. Also in this section are other contributions which did not fit into the anthology but are nonetheless of interest.

Bible Readings

THE SENTENCES

ST JOHN 11: 25–26

I am the resurrection and the life, saith the Lord: he that believeth in me, though he were dead, yet shall he live: and whosoever liveth and believeth in me shall never die.

JOB 19: 25–27

I know that my Redeemer liveth, and that he shall stand at the latter day upon the earth: and though after my skin worms destroy this body, yet in my flesh shall I see God; whom I shall see for myself, and mine eyes shall behold, and not another.

1 TIMOTHY 6: 7; JOB 1: 21

We brought nothing into this world, and it is certain we can carry nothing out. The Lord gave, and the Lord hath taken away; blessed be the name of the Lord.

The darkness is no darkness with thee, but the night is as clear as the day: the darkness and the light to thee are both alike.

The eternal God is thy refuge, and underneath are the everlasting arms.

The souls of the righteous are in the hand of God.

THE READINGS

ECCLESIASTES 3: 1–11

To every thing there is a season, and a time to every purpose under the heaven: a time to be born, and a time to die; a time to plant, and a time to pluck up that which is planted; a time to kill, and a time to heal; a time to break down, and a time to build up; a time to weep, and a time to laugh; a time to mourn, and a time to dance; a time to cast away stones, and a time to gather stones together; a time to embrace, and a time to refrain from embracing; a time to get, and a time to lose; a time to keep, and a time to cast away; a time to rend, and a time to sew; a time to keep silence, and a time to speak; a time to love, and a time to hate; a time of war, and a time of peace. What profit hath he that worketh in that wherein he laboureth? I have seen the travail, which God hath given to the sons of men to be exercised in it. He hath made every thing beautiful in his time: also he hath set the world in their heart, so that no man can find out the work that God maketh from the beginning to the end.

ROMANS 8: 14–25

For all who are led by the Spirit of God are sons of God. The Spirit you have received is not a spirit of slavery, leading you back into a life of fear, but a Spirit of adoption, enabling us to cry 'Abba! Father!' The Spirit of God affirms to our spirit that we are God's children; and if children, then heirs, heirs of God and fellow-heirs with Christ; but we must share his sufferings if we are also to share his glory. For I reckon that the sufferings we now endure bear no comparison with the glory, as yet unrevealed, which is in store for us. The created universe is waiting with eager expectation for God's sons to be revealed. It was made subject to frustration, not of its own choice but by the will of him who subjected it, yet with the hope that the universe itself is to be freed from the shackles of mortality and is to enter upon the glorious liberty of the children of God. Up to the present, as we know, the whole created universe in all its parts groans as if in the pangs of childbirth. What is more, we also, to whom the Spirit is given as the first-fruits of the harvest to come, are groaning inwardly while we look forward eagerly to our adoption, our liberation from mortality. It was with this hope that we were saved. Now to see something is no longer to hope: why hope for what is already seen? But if we hope for something we do not yet see, then we look forward to it eagerly and with patience.

ROMANS 8: 31–39

What shall we then say to these things? If God be for us, who can be against us? He that spared not his own Son, but delivered him up for us all, how shall he not with him also freely give us all things? Who shall lay any thing to the charge of God's elect? It is God that justifieth. Who is he that condemneth? It is Christ that died, yea rather, that is risen again, who is even at the right hand of God, who also maketh intercession for us. Who shall separate us from the love of Christ? shall tribulation, or distress, or persecution, or famine, or nakedness, or peril, or sword? As it is written, for thy sake we are killed all the day long; we are accounted as sheep for the slaughter. Nay, in all these things we are more than conquerors through him that loved us. For I am persuaded, that neither death, nor life, nor angels, nor principalities, nor powers, nor things present, nor things to come, nor height, nor depth, nor any other creature, shall be able to separate us from the love of God, which is in Christ Jesus our Lord.

1 CORINTHIANS 13

Though I speak with the tongues of men and of angels, and have not charity, I am become as sounding brass, or a tinkling cymbal. And though I have the gift of prophecy, and understand all mysteries and all knowledge; and though I have all faith, so that I could remove mountains, and have not charity, I am nothing. And though I bestow all my goods to feed the poor, and though I give my body to be burned, and have not charity, it profiteth me nothing. Charity suffereth long, and is kind; charity envieth not; charity vaunteth not itself, is not puffed up, doth not behave itself unseemly, seeketh not her own, is not easily provoked, thinketh no evil; rejoiceth not in iniquity, but rejoiceth in the truth; beareth all things, believeth all things, hopeth all things, endureth all things. Charity never faileth: but whether there be prophecies, they shall fail; whether there be tongues, they shall cease; whether there be knowledge, it shall vanish away. For we know in part, and we prophesy in part. But when that which is perfect is come, then that which is in part shall be done away. When I was a child, I spake as a child, I understood as a child, I thought as a child: but when I became a man, I put away childish things. For now we see through a glass, darkly; but then face to face: now I know in part; but then shall I know even as also I am known. And now abideth faith, hope, charity, these three; but the greatest of these is charity.

St John 14: 1–14

Jesus said: 'Let not your heart be troubled: ye believe in God, believe also in me. In my Father's house are many mansions: if it were not so, I would have told you. I go to prepare a place for you. And if I go and prepare a place for you, I will come again, and receive you unto myself; that where I am, there ye may be also. And whither I go ye know, and the way ye know.' Thomas saith unto him, 'Lord, we know not whither thou goest; and how can we know the way?' Jesus saith unto him, 'I am the way, the truth, and the life: no man cometh unto the Father, but by me. If ye had known me, ye should have known my Father also: and from henceforth ye know him, and have seen him.' Philip saith unto him, 'Lord, shew us the Father, and it sufficeth us.' Jesus saith unto him, 'Have I been so long time with you, and yet hast thou not known me, Philip? he that hath seen me hath seen the Father; and how sayest thou then, shew us the Father? Believest thou not that I am in the Father, and the Father in me? the words that I speak unto you I speak not of myself: but the Father that dwelleth in me, he doeth the works. Believe me that I am in the Father, and the Father in me: or else believe me for the very works' sake. Verily, verily, I say unto you, He that believeth in me, the works that I do shall he do also; and greater works than these shall he do; because I go unto my Father. And whatsoever ye shall ask in my name, that will I do, that the Father may be glorified in the Son. If ye shall ask any thing in my name, I will do it.'

Revelation 21: 1–7

And I saw a new heaven and a new earth: for the first heaven and the first earth were passed away; and there was no more sea. And I John saw the holy city, new Jerusalem, coming down from God out of heaven, prepared as a bride adorned for her husband. And I heard a great voice out of heaven saying, Behold, the tabernacle of God is with men, and he will dwell with them, and they shall be his people, and God himself shall be with them, and be their God. And God shall wipe away all tears from their eyes; and there shall be no more death, neither sorrow, nor crying, neither shall there be any more pain: for the former things are passed away. And he that sat upon the throne said, Behold, I make all things new. And he said unto me, Write: for these words are true and faithful. And he said unto me, It is done. I am Alpha and Omega, the beginning and the end. I will give unto him that is athirst of the fountain of the water of life freely. He that overcometh shall inherit all things; and I will be his God, and he shall be my son.

PSALM 121

I will lift up mine eyes unto the hills, from whence cometh my help.
My help cometh even from the Lord, who hath made heaven and earth.
He will not suffer thy foot to be moved: and he that keepeth thee will not sleep.
Behold, he that keepeth Israel shall neither slumber nor sleep.
The Lord himself is thy keeper: the Lord is thy defence upon thy right hand;
So that the sun shall not burn thee by day, neither the moon by night.
The Lord shall preserve thee from all evil: yea, it is even he that shall keep thy soul.
The Lord shall preserve thy going out, and thy coming in, from this time forth for evermore.
Glory be to the Father, and to the Son, and to the Holy Ghost;
As it was in the beginning, is now, and ever shall be, world without end. Amen.

I CORINTHIANS 15: 20–26, 35–38, 42–45, 53–58

Now is Christ risen from the dead, and become the firstfruits of them that slept. For since by man came death, by man came also the resurrection of the dead. For as in Adam all die, even so in Christ shall all be made alive. But every man in his own order: Christ the firstfruits;

afterward they that are Christ's at his coming. Then cometh the end, when he shall have delivered up the kingdom to God, even the Father; when he shall have put down all rule and all authority and power. For he must reign, till he hath put all enemies under his feet. The last enemy that shall be destroyed is death.

But someone will say, How are the dead raised up? and with what body do they come? Thou fool, that which thou sowest is not quickened, except it die. And that which thou sowest, thou sowest not that body that shall be, but bare grain, it may chance of wheat, or of some other grain. But God giveth it a body as it hath pleased him, and to every seed his own body.

So also is the resurrection of the dead. It is sown in corruption; it is raised in incorruption. It is sown in dishonour; it is raised in glory: it is sown in weakness; it is raised in power. It is sown a natural body; it is raised a spiritual body.

For this corruptible must put on incorruption, and this mortal must put on immortality. So when this corruptible shall have put on incorruption, and this mortal shall have put on immortality, then shall be brought to pass the saying that is written, Death is swallowed up in victory. O death, where is thy sting? O grave, where is thy victory? The sting of death is sin; and the strength of sin is the law. But thanks be to God, which giveth us the victory through our Lord Jesus Christ. Therefore, my beloved brethren, be ye steadfast, unmoveable, always abounding in the work of the Lord, forasmuch as ye know that your labour is not in vain in the Lord.

II CORINTHIANS 3: 7–9, 18; 4: 1–8

If the ministration of death, written and engraven in stones, was glorious, so that the children of Israel could not stedfastly behold the face of Moses for the glory of his countenance, which glory was to be done away: How shall not the ministration of the spirit be rather glorious? For if the ministration of condemnation be glory, much more doth the ministration of righteousness exceed in glory. We all, with open face beholding as in a glass the glory of the Lord, are changed into the same image from glory to glory, even as by the Spirit of the Lord.

Therefore seeing we have this ministry, as we have received mercy, we faint not: but have renounced the hidden things of dishonesty, not walking in craftiness, nor handling the word of God deceitfully; but by manifestation of the truth commending ourselves to every man's conscience in the sight of God. For we preach not ourselves, but Christ Jesus the Lord; and ourselves your servants for Jesus' sake. For God, who commanded the light to shine out of darkness, hath shined in our hearts, to give the light of the knowledge of the glory of God in the face of Jesus Christ. But we have this treasure in earthen vessels, that the excellency of the power may be of God, and not of us.

ECCLESIASTICUS 44: 1–15

Let us now praise famous men, and our fathers that begat us. The Lord hath wrought great glory by them through his great power from the beginning. Such as did bear rule in their kingdoms, men renowned for their power, giving counsel by their understanding, and declaring prophecies: leaders of the people by their counsels, and by their knowledge of learning meet for the people, wise and eloquent in their instructions: such as found out musical tunes, and recited verses in writing: rich men furnished with ability, living peaceably in their habitations: all these were honoured in their generations, and were the glory of their times. There be of them, that have left a name behind them, that their praises might be reported. And some there be, which have no memorial; who are perished, as though they had never been; and are become as though they had never been born; and their children after them. But these were merciful men, whose righteousness hath not been forgotten. With their seed shall continually remain a good inheritance, and their children are within the covenant. Their seed standeth fast, and their children for their sakes. Their seed shall remain for ever, and their glory shall not be blotted out. Their bodies are buried in peace; but their name liveth for evermore. The people will tell of their wisdom, and the congregation will shew forth their praise.

EPHESIANS 1: 1–14

Paul, an apostle of Jesus Christ by the will of God, to the saints which are at Ephesus, and to the faithful in Christ Jesus: Grace be to you, and peace, from God our Father, and from the Lord Jesus Christ. Blessed be the God and Father of our Lord Jesus Christ, who hath blessed us with all spiritual blessings in heavenly places in Christ: according as he hath chosen us in him before the foundation of the world, that we should be holy and without blame before him in love: having predestinated us unto the adoption of children by Jesus Christ to himself, according to the good pleasure of his will, to the praise of the glory of his grace, wherein he hath made us accepted in the beloved. In whom we have redemption through his blood, the forgiveness of sins, according to the riches of his grace; wherein he hath abounded toward us in all wisdom and prudence; having made known unto us the mystery of his will, according to his good pleasure which he hath purposed in himself: that in the dispensation of the fulness of times he might gather together in one all things in Christ, both which are in heaven, and which are on earth; even in him: in whom also we have obtained an inheritance, being predestinated according to the purpose of him who worketh all things after the counsel of his own will: that we should be to the praise of his glory, who first trusted in Christ. In whom ye also trusted, after that ye heard the word of truth, the gospel of your salvation: in whom also after that ye believed, ye were sealed with that holy Spirit of promise, which is the earnest of our inheritance until the redemption of the purchased possession, unto the praise of his glory.

EPHESIANS 6: 10–18

Finally, my brethren, be strong in the Lord, and in the power of his might. Put on the whole armour of God, that ye may be able to stand against the wiles of the devil. For we wrestle not against flesh and blood, but against principalities, against powers, against the rulers of the darkness of this world, against spiritual wickedness in high places. Wherefore take unto you the whole armour of God, that ye may be able to withstand in the evil day, and having done all, to stand. Stand therefore, having your loins girt about with truth, and having on the breastplate of righteousness; and your feet shod with the preparation of the gospel of peace; above all, taking the shield of faith, wherewith ye shall be able to quench all the fiery darts of the wicked. And take the helmet of salvation, and the sword of the Spirit, which is the word of God: praying always with all prayer and supplication in the Spirit, and watching thereunto with all perseverance and supplication for all saints.

HEBREWS 11: 1–8

Now faith is the substance of things hoped for, the evidence of things not seen. For by it the elders obtained a good report. Through faith we understand that the worlds were framed by the word of God, so that things which are seen were not made of things which do appear. By faith Abel offered unto God a more excellent sacrifice than Cain, by which he obtained witness that he was righteous, God testifying of his gifts: and by it he being dead yet speaketh. By faith Enoch was translated that he should not see death; and was not found, because God had translated him: for before his translation he had this testimony, that he pleased God. But without faith it is impossible to please him: for he that cometh to God must believe that he is, and that he is a rewarder of them that diligently seek him. By faith Noah, being warned of God of things not seen as yet, moved with fear, prepared an ark to the saving of his house; by the which he condemned the world, and became heir of the righteousness which is by faith. By faith Abraham when he was called to go out into a place which he should after receive for an inheritance, obeyed; and he went out, not knowing whither he went.

ISAIAH 61: 1–4; 10–11

The Spirit of the Lord God is upon me; because the Lord hath anointed me to preach good tidings unto the meek; he hath sent me to bind up the broken-hearted, to proclaim liberty to the captives, and the opening of the prison to them that are bound; to proclaim the acceptable year of the Lord, and the day of vengeance of our God; to comfort all that mourn; to appoint unto them that mourn in Zion, to give unto them beauty for ashes, the oil of joy for mourning, the garment of praise for the spirit of heaviness; that they might be called trees of righteousness, the planting of the Lord, that he might be glorified. And they shall build the old wastes, they shall raise up the former desolations, and they shall repair the waste cities, the desolations of many generations.

I will greatly rejoice in the Lord, my soul shall be joyful in my God. For as the earth bringeth forth her bud, and as the garden causeth the things that are sown in it to spring forth; so the Lord God will cause righteousness and praise to spring forth before all the nations.

St John 1: 1–18

In the beginning was the Word, and the Word was with God, and the Word was God. The same was in the beginning with God. All things were made by him; and without him was not any thing made that was made. In him was life; and the life was the light of men. And the light shineth in darkness; and the darkness comprehended it not. There was a man sent from God, whose name was John. The same came for a witness, to bear witness of the Light, that all men through him might believe. He was not that Light, but was sent to bear witness of that Light. That was the true Light, which lighteth every man that cometh into the world. He was in the world, and the world was made by him, and the world knew him not. He came unto his own, and his own received him not. But as many as received him, to them gave he power to become the sons of God, even to them that believe on his name: which were born, not of blood, nor of the will of the flesh, nor of the will of man, but of God. And the Word was made flesh, and dwelt among us, (and we beheld his glory, the glory as of the only begotten of the Father,) full of grace and truth. John bare witness of him, and cried, saying, This was he of whom I spake, He that cometh after me is preferred before me: for he was before me. And of his fulness have all we received, and grace for grace. For the law was given by Moses, but grace and truth came by Jesus Christ. No man hath seen God at any time; the only begotten Son, which is in the bosom of the Father, he hath declared him.

[12]

St Mark 9: 2–8

And after six days Jesus taketh with him Peter, and James, and John, and leadeth them up into an high mountain apart by themselves: and he was transfigured before them. And his raiment became shining, exceeding white as snow; so as no fuller on earth can white them. And there appeared unto them Elias with Moses: and they were talking with Jesus. And Peter answered and said to Jesus, Master, it is good for us to be here: and let us make three tabernacles; one for thee, and one for Moses, and one for Elias. For he wist not what to say; for they were sore afraid. And there was a cloud that overshadowed them: and a voice came out of the cloud, saying, This is my beloved Son: hear him. And suddenly, when they had looked round about, they saw no man any more, save only Jesus with themselves.

I Thessalonians 4: 13–18

Brethren: We will not have you ignorant concerning them that are asleep, that you be not sorrowful, even as others who have no hope; for if we believe that Jesus died and rose again, even so them who have slept through Jesus, will God bring with Him. For this we say unto you in the word of the Lord, that we who are alive, who remain unto the coming of the Lord, shall not prevent them who have slept. For the Lord Himself shall come down from heaven, with commandment, and with the voice of an Arch-angel, and with the trumpet of God; and the dead who are in Christ shall rise first. Then we who are alive, who are left, shall be taken up together with them in the clouds to meet Christ, into the air, and so shall we be always with the Lord. Wherefore comfort ye one another with these words.

Philippians 2: 1–11

If there is any encouragement in Christ, any incentive of love, any participation in the Spirit, any affection and sympathy, complete my joy by being of the same mind, having the same love, being in full accord and of one mind. Do nothing from selfishness or conceit, but in humility count others better than yourselves. Let each of you look not only to his own interests, but also to the interests of others. Have this mind among yourselves, which is yours in Christ Jesus, who, though he was in the form of God, did not count equality with God a thing to be grasped, but emptied himself, taking the form of a servant, being born in the likeness of men. And being found in human form he humbled himself and became obedient unto death, even death on a cross. Therefore God has highly exalted him and bestowed on him the name which is above every name, that at the name of Jesus every knee should bow, in heaven and on earth and under the earth, and every tongue confess that Jesus Christ is Lord, to the glory of God the Father.

PHILIPPIANS 4: 4–9

Rejoice in the Lord always; again I will say, Rejoice. Let all men know your forbearance. The Lord is at hand. Have no anxiety about anything, but in every thing by prayer and supplication with thanksgiving let your requests be made known to God. And the peace of God, which passes all understanding, will keep your hearts and your minds in Christ Jesus. Finally, brethren, whatever is true, whatever is honourable, whatever is just, whatever is pure, whatever is lovely, whatever is gracious, if there is any excellence, if there is anything worthy of praise, think about these things. What you have learned and received and heard and seen in me, do; and the God of peace will be with you.

PSALM 104: 1–12

Bless the Lord, my soul: O Lord my God, thou art great indeed, clothed in majesty and splendour, and wrapped in a robe of light. Thou hast spread out the heavens like a tent and on their waters laid the beams of thy pavilion; who takest the clouds for thy chariot, riding on the wings of the wind; who makest the winds thy messengers and flames of fire thy servants; thou didst fix the earth on its foundation so that it never can be shaken; the deep overspread it like a cloak, and the waters lay above the mountains. At thy rebuke they ran, at the sound of thy thunder they rushed away, flowing over the hills, pouring down into the valleys to the place appointed for them. Thou didst fix a boundary which they might not pass; they shall not return to cover the earth.

Thou dost make springs break out in the gullies, so that their waters run between the hills. The wild beasts all drink from them, the wild asses quench their thirst; the birds of the air nest on their banks and sing among the leaves.

PSALM 84

How amiable are thy tabernacles, O Lord of hosts! My soul longeth, yea, even fainteth for the courts of the Lord: my heart and my flesh crieth out for the living God. Yea, the sparrow hath found an house, and the swallow a nest for herself, where she may lay her young, even thine altars, O Lord of hosts, my King, and my God. Blessed are they that dwell in thy house: they will be still praising thee. Selah. Blessed is the man whose strength is in thee; in whose heart are the ways of them. Who passing through the valley of Baca make it a well; the rain also filleth the pools. They go from strength to strength, every one of them in Zion appeareth before God. O Lord God of hosts, hear my prayer: give ear, O God of Jacob. Selah. Behold, O God our shield, and look upon the face of thine anointed. For a day in thy courts is better than a thousand. I had rather be a doorkeeper in the house of my God, than to dwell in the tents of wickedness. For the Lord God is a sun and shield: the Lord will give grace and glory: no good thing will he withhold from them that walk uprightly. O Lord of hosts, blessed is the man that trusteth in thee.

PSALM 91

He that dwelleth in the secret place of the most High shall abide under the shadow of the Almighty. I will say of the Lord, He is my refuge and my fortress: my God; in him will I trust. Surely he shall deliver thee from the snare of the fowler, and from the noisome pestilence. He shall cover thee with his feathers, and under his wings shalt thou trust: his truth shall be thy shield and buckler. Thou shalt not be afraid for the terror by night; nor for the arrow that flieth by day; nor for the pestilence that walketh in darkness; nor for the destruction that wasteth at noonday. A thousand shall fall at thy side, and ten thousand at thy right hand; but it shall not come nigh thee. Only with thine eyes shalt thou behold and see the reward of the wicked. Because thou hast made the Lord, which is my refuge, even the most High, thy habitation; there shall no evil befall thee, neither shall any plague come nigh thy dwelling. For he shall give his angels charge over thee, to keep thee in all thy ways. They shall bear thee up in their hands, lest thou dash thy foot against a stone. Thou shalt tread upon the lion and adder: the young lion and the dragon shalt thou trample under feet. Because he hath set his love upon me, therefore will I deliver him: I will set him on high, because he hath known my name. He shall call upon me, and I will answer him: I will be with him in trouble; I will deliver him, and honour him. With long life will I satisfy him, and shew him my salvation.

PSALM 139

O Lord, thou hast searched me, and known me. Thou knowest my down-sitting and mine uprising, thou understandest my thought afar off. Thou compassest my path and my lying down, and art acquainted with all my ways. For there is not a word in my tongue, but, lo, O Lord, thou knowest it altogether. Thou hast beset me behind and before, and laid thine hand upon me. Such knowledge is too wonderful for me; it is high, I cannot attain unto it. Whither shall I go from thy spirit? or whither shall I flee from thy presence? If I ascend up into heaven, thou art there: if I make my bed in hell, behold, thou art there. If I take the wings of the morning, and dwell in the uttermost parts of the sea; even there shall thy hand lead me, and thy right hand shall hold me. If I say, Surely the darkness shall cover me; even the night shall be light about me. Yea, the darkness hideth not from thee; but the night shineth as the day: the darkness and the light are both alike to thee. For thou hast possessed my reins: thou hast covered me in my mother's womb. I will praise thee; for I am fearfully and wonderfully made: marvellous are thy works; and that my soul knoweth right well. My substance was not hid from thee, when I was made in secret, and curiously wrought in the lowest parts of the earth. Thine eyes did see my substance, yet being unperfect; and in thy book all my members were written, which in continuance were fashioned, when as yet there was none of them. How precious also are thy thoughts unto me, O God! how great is the sum of them! If I should count them, they are more in number than the sand: when I awake, I am still with thee. Surely thou wilt slay the wicked, O God: depart from me therefore, ye bloody men. For they speak against thee wickedly, and thine enemies take thy name in vain. Do not I hate them, O Lord, that hate thee? and am not I grieved with those that rise up against thee? I hate them with perfect hatred: I count them mine enemies. Search me, O God, and know my heart: try me, and know my thoughts: And see if there be any wicked way in me, and lead me in the way everlasting.

PSALM 142

I cried unto the Lord with my voice: yea, even unto the Lord did I make my supplication. I poured out my complaints before him, and shewed him of my trouble. When my spirit was in heaviness thou knewest my path: in the way wherein I walked have they privily laid a snare for me. I looked also upon my right hand, and saw there was no man that would know me. I had no place to flee unto, and no man cared for my soul. I cried unto thee, O Lord, and said: Thou art my hope, and my portion in the land of the living. Consider my complaint, for I am brought very low. O deliver me from my persecutors, for they are too strong for me. Bring my soul out of prison, that I may give thanks unto thy Name: which thing if thou wilt grant me, then shall the righteous resort unto my company.

PROVERBS 3: 1–12

My son, forget not my law; but let thine heart keep my commandments: for length of days, and long life, and peace, shall they add to thee. Let not mercy and truth forsake thee: bind them about thy neck; write them upon the table of thine heart: so shalt thou find favour and good understanding in the sight of God and man. Trust in the Lord with all thine heart; and lean not unto thine own understanding. In all thy ways acknowledge him, and he shall direct thy paths. Be not wise in thine own eyes: fear the Lord, and depart from evil. It shall be health to thy navel, and marrow to thy bones. Honour the Lord with thy substance, and with the firstfruits of all thine increase: so shall thy barns be filled with plenty, and thy presses shall burst out with new wine. My son, despise not the chastening of the Lord; neither be weary of his correction: for whom the Lord loveth he correcteth; even as a father the son in whom he delighteth.

PROVERBS 3: 13–17

Happy is the man that findeth wisdom, and the man that getteth understanding. For the merchandise of it is better than the merchandise of silver, and the gain thereof than fine gold. She is more precious than rubies: and all the things thou canst desire are not to be compared unto her. Length of days is in her right hand; and in her left hand riches and honour. Her ways are ways of pleasantness, and all her paths are peace.

REVELATION 7: 9–17

After this I beheld, and, lo, a great multitude, which no man could number, of all nations, and kindreds, and people, and tongues, stood before the throne, and before the Lamb, clothed with white robes, and palms in their hands; and cried with a loud voice, saying, Salvation to our God which sitteth upon the throne, and unto the Lamb. And all the angels stood round about the throne, and about the elders and the four beasts, and fell before the throne on their faces, and worshipped God, saying, Amen: Blessing, and glory, and wisdom, and thanks-giving, and honour, and power, and might, be unto our God for ever and ever. Amen. And one of the elders answered, saying unto me, What are these which are arrayed in white robes? and whence came they? And I said unto him, Sir, thou knowest. And he said to me, These are they which came out of great tribulation, and have washed their robes, and made them white in the blood of the Lamb. Therefore are they before the throne of God, and serve him day and night in his temple: and he that sitteth on the throne shall dwell among them. They shall hunger no more, neither thirst any more; neither shall the sun light on them, nor any heat. For the Lamb which is in the midst of the throne shall feed them, and shall lead them unto living fountains of waters: and God shall wipe away all tears from their eyes.

WISDOM 7: 15, 8: 1

May God grant that I speak with judgement and have thoughts worthy of what I have received, for he is the guide even of wisdom and the corrector of the wise. For both we and our words are in his hand, as are all understanding and skill in crafts. For it is he who gave me unerring knowledge of what exists, to know the structure of the world and the activity of the elements; the beginning and end and middle of times, the alternations of the solstices and the changes of the seasons, the cycles of the year and the constellations of the stars, the natures of animals and the tempers of wild beasts, the powers of spirits and the reasonings of men, the varieties of plants and the virtues of roots; I learned both what is secret and what is manifest, for wisdom, the fashioner of all things, taught me.

For in her there is a spirit that is intelligent, holy, unique, manifold, subtle, mobile, clear, unpolluted, distinct, invulnerable, loving the good, keen, irresistible, beneficent, humane, steadfast, sure, free from anxiety, all-powerful, overseeing all, and penetrating through all spirits that are intelligent and pure and most subtle. For wisdom is more mobile than any motion; because of her pureness she pervades and penetrates all things. For she is a breath of the power of God, and a pure emanation of the glory of the Almighty; therefore nothing defiled gains entrance into her. For she is a reflection of eternal light, a spotless mirror of the working of God, and an image of his goodness. Though she is but one, she can do all things, and while remaining in herself, she renews all things; in every generation she passes into holy souls and makes them friends of God, and prophets; for God loves nothing so much as the man who lives with wisdom. For she is more beautiful than the sun, and excels every constellation of the stars. Compared with the light she is found to be superior, for it is succeeded by the night, but against wisdom evil does not prevail. She reaches mightily from one end of the earth to the other, and she orders all things well.

Proverbs 4: 4–13

Let thine heart retain my words: keep my commandments, and live. Get wisdom, get understanding: forget it not: neither decline from the words of my mouth. Forsake her not, and she shall preserve thee: love her, and she shall keep thee. Wisdom is the principal thing; therefore get wisdom: and with all thy getting get understanding. Exalt her, and she shall promote thee: she shall bring thee to honour, when thou dost embrace her. She shall give to thine head an ornament of grace: a crown of glory shall she deliver to thee. Hear, O my son, and receive my sayings; and the years of thy life shall be many. I have taught thee in the way of wisdom; I have led thee in right paths. When thou goest, thy steps shall not be straitened; and when thou runnest, thou shalt not stumble. Take fast hold of instruction: let her not go: keep her; for she is thy life.

Poems

from CYMBELINE

Fear no more the heat o'the sun,
  Nor the furious winter's rages;
Thou thy worldly task hast done,
  Home art gone, and ta'en thy wages:
Golden lads and girls all must,
  As chimney-sweepers, come to dust.

Fear no more the frown o'the great,
  Thou art past the tyrant's stroke:
Care no more to clothe and eat;
  To thee the reed is as the oak;
The sceptre, learning, physic, must
  All follow this, and come to dust.

Fear no more the lightning-flash,
  Nor the all-dreaded thunder-stone;
Fear not slander, censure rash;
  Thou hast finish'd joy and moan:
All lovers young, all lovers must
  Consign to thee, and come to dust.

No exorciser harm thee!
  Nor no witchcraft charm thee!
Ghost unlaid forbear thee!
  Nothing ill come near thee!
Quiet consummation have;
  And renowned be thy grave!

WILLIAM SHAKESPEARE

The owl and the pussy-cat

The Owl and the Pussy-cat went to sea
  In a beautiful pea-green boat,
They took some honey, and plenty of money,
  Wrapped up in a five-pound note.

[23]

The Owl looked up to the stars above,
    And sang to a small guitar,
'O lovely Pussy! O Pussy, my love,
    What a beautiful Pussy you are,
        You are,
        You are!
    What a beautiful Pussy you are!'

Pussy said to the Owl, 'You elegant fowl!
    How charmingly sweet you sing!
O let us be married! too long we have tarried:
    But what shall we do for a ring?'
They sailed away, for a year and a day,
    To the land where the Bong-tree grows,
And there in a wood a Piggy-wig stood,
    With a ring at the end of his nose,
        His nose,
        His nose,
    With a ring at the end of his nose.

'Dear Pig, are you willing to sell for one shilling
    Your ring?' Said the Piggy, 'I will.'
So they took it away, and were married next day
    By the Turkey who lives on the hill.
They dined on mince, and slices of quince,
    Which they ate with a runcible spoon;
And hand in hand, on the edge of the sand,
    They danced by the light of the moon,
        The moon,
        The moon,
    They danced by the light of the moon.

EDWARD LEAR

'The dead are not under the earth'

The dead are not under the earth
They are in the tree that rustles
They are in the woods that groan
They are in the water that runs
They are in the water that sleeps

They are in the hut, they are in the crowd
The dead are not dead.
Those who are dead are never gone
They are in the breast of a woman
They are in the child that is wailing and in the fire that flames.
   The dead are not under the earth
They are in the fire that is dying
They are in the grass that is weeping
They are in the whimpering rocks
They are in the forest, they are in the house
They are not dead.

When my ancestors talk about the Creator they say: He is with us . . . We
sleep with him. We hunt with him. We dance with him.

FRANCIS NNAGGENDA

❧

from ANTONY AND CLEOPATRA

So, fare thee well.
 Now boast thee, death, in thy possession lies
A lass unparallel'd. Downy windows, close;
And golden Phoebus never be beheld
Of eyes again so royal!
         She looks like sleep,
As she would catch another Antony
In her strong toil of grace.

WILLIAM SHAKESPEARE

❧

from THE TEMPEST

Our revels now are ended. These our actors,
As I foretold you, were all spirits, and
Are melted into air, into thin air;
And like the baseless fabric of this vision,

The cloud-capped towers, the gorgeous palaces,
The solemn temples, the great globe itself,
Yea, all which it inherit, shall dissolve;
And, like this insubstantial pageant faded,
Leave not a rack behind. We are such stuff
As dreams are made on, and our little life
Is rounded with a sleep.

WILLIAM SHAKESPEARE

The path

O Lord, in whom I've sought to disbelieve,
    Look upon me.
Fortify an atheist's lack of faith.
    Look upon me.

BRIAN ALDISS

Do not be afraid

Do not stand at my grave and weep
I am not there, I do not sleep.
I am a thousand winds that blow,
I am the diamond glint on snow.
I am the sunlight on ripened grain,
I am the gentle autumn rain.
When you wake in the morning hush
I am the swift, uplifting rush
of quiet birds in circling flight,
I am the soft starlight at night,
Do not stand at my grave and weep
·I am not there – I do not sleep.

AMERICAN INDIAN

'I have seen death too often'

I have seen death too often to believe in death.
It is not an ending, but a withdrawal.
As one who finishes a long journey
Stills the motor, turns off the lights,
Steps from his car,
And walks up the path to the home that awaits him.

ANON.

'I shall go without companions'

I shall go without companions,
And with nothing in my hand
I shall pass through many places,
That I cannot understand
Until I come to my own country,
Which is a pleasant land.

The trees that grow in my own country
Are the beech-tree and the yew;
Many stand together and some stand few.
In the month of May in my own country
All the woods are new.

When I get to my own country
I shall lie down and sleep;
I shall watch in the valleys the long flocks of sheep
And then I shall dream for ever and all
A good dream and deep.

HILAIRE BELLOC

Jim

There was a Boy whose name was Jim;
His Friends were very good to him.
They gave him Tea, and Cakes, and Jam.
And slices of delicious Ham,
And Chocolate with pink inside,
And little Tricycles to ride,
And read him Stories through and through,
And even took him to the Zoo —
But there it was the dreadful Fate
Befell him, which I now relate.

You know — at least you ought to know,
For I have often told you so —
That Children never are allowed
To leave their Nurses in a Crowd;
Now this was Jim's especial Foible,
He ran away when he was able,
And on this inauspicious day
He slipped his hand and ran away!

He hadn't gone a yard when — Bang!
With open Jaws, a Lion sprang,
And hungrily began to eat
The Boy: beginning at his feet.
Now, just imagine how it feels
When first your toes and then your heels,
And then by gradual degrees,
Your shins and ankles, calves and knees,
Are slowly eaten, bit by bit.
No wonder Jim detested it!
No wonder that he shouted 'Hi!'

The Honest Keeper heard his cry,
Though very fat he almost ran
To help the little gentleman.
'Ponto!' he ordered as he came
(For Ponto was the Lion's name),
'Ponto!' he cried, with angry Frown,
'Let go, Sir! Down, Sir! Put it down!'

The Lion made a sudden stop,
He let the Dainty Morsel drop,
And slunk reluctant to his Cage,
Snarling with Disappointed Rage.
But when he bent him over Jim,
The Honest Keeper's Eyes were dim.
The Lion having reached his Head,
The Miserable Boy was dead!

When Nurse informed his Parents, they
Were more Concerned than I can say: —
His Mother, as she dried her eyes,
Said, 'Well — it gives me no surprise,
He would not do as he was told!'
His Father, who was self-controlled,
Bade all the children round attend
To James's miserable end,
And always keep a-hold of Nurse
For fear of finding something worse.

HILAIRE BELLOC

Lord Hippo

Lord Hippo suffered fearful loss
By putting money on a horse
Which he believed, if it were pressed,
Would run far faster than the rest:
For someone who was in the know
Had confidently told him so.
But on the morning of the race
It only took the *seventh* place!
Picture the Viscount's great surprise!
He scarcely could believe his eyes!
He sought the Individual who
Had laid him odds at 9 to 2,
Suggesting as a useful tip
That they should enter Partnership

And put to joint account the debt
Arising from his foolish bet.
But when the Bookie – oh! my word,
I only wish you could have heard
The way he roared he did not think,
And hoped that they might strike him pink!
Lord Hippo simply turned and ran
From this infuriated man.
Despairing, maddened and distraught
He utterly collapsed and sought
His sire, the Earl of Potamus,
And brokenly addressed him thus:
'Dread Sire – to-day – at Ascot – I . . .'
His genial parent made reply:
'Come! Come! Come! Come! Don't look so glum!
Trust your Papa and name the sum . . .
What? . . . Fifteen hundred thousand? . . . Hum!
However . . . stiffen up, you wreck;
Boys will be boys – so here's the cheque!'
Lord Hippo, feeling deeply – well,
More grateful than he cared to tell –
Punted the lot on Little Nell: –
And got a telegram at dinner
To say that he had backed the Winner!

HILAIRE BELLOC

South London Sketch, 1844

Lavender Sweep is drowned in Wandsworth,
    Drowned in jessamine up to the neck,
Beetles sway upon bending grass leagues
    Shoulder-level to Tooting Bec.
Rich as Middlesex, rich in signboards,
    Lie the lover-trod lanes between,
Red Man, Green Man, Horse and Waggoner,
    Elms and sycamores round a green.

Burst, good June, with a rush this morning,
    Bindweed weave me an emerald rope
Sun, shine bright on the blossoming trellises,
    June and lavender, bring me hope.

JOHN BETJEMAN

Trebetherick

We used to picnic where the thrift
    Grew deep and tufted to the edge;
We saw the yellow foam-flakes drift
    In trembling sponges on the ledge
Below us, till the wind would lift
    Them up the cliff and o'er the hedge.
Sand in the sandwiches, wasps in the tea,
Sun on our bathing-dresses heavy with the wet,
Squelch of the bladder-wrack waiting for the sea,
Fleas round the tamarisk, an early cigarette.

From where the coastguard houses stood
    One used to see, below the hill,
The lichened branches of a wood
    In summer silver-cool and still;
And there the Shade of Evil could
    Stretch out at us from Shilla Mill.
Thick with sloe and blackberry, uneven in the light,
Lonely ran the hedge, the heavy meadow was remote,
The oldest part of Cornwall was the wood as black as night,
And the pheasant and the rabbit lay torn open at the throat.

But when a storm was at its height,
    And feathery slate was black in rain,
And tamarisks were hung with light
    And golden sand was brown again,
Spring tide and blizzard would unite
    And sea came flooding up the lane.

Waves full of treasure then were roaring up the beach,
Ropes round our mackintoshes, waders warm and dry,
We waited for the wreckage to come swirling into reach,
Ralph, Vasey, Alastair, Biddy, John and I.

    Then roller into roller curled
        And thundered down the rocky bay,
    And we were in a water-world
        Of rain and blizzard, sea and spray,
    And one against the other hurled
        We struggled round to Greenaway.
Blessèd be St Enodoc, blessèd be the wave,
Blessèd be the springy turf, we pray, pray to thee,
Ask for our children all the happy days you gave
To Ralph, Vasey, Alastair, Biddy, John and me.

JOHN BETJEMAN

✦

The ship

What is dying?
I am standing in the sea shore,
a ship sails to the morning breeze
and starts for the ocean.
She is an object of beauty
and I stand watching her
till at last she fades
on the horizon
and someone at my side says,
'She is gone'.
Gone! Where?
Gone from my sight – that is all.
She is just as large in the masts, hull and spars
as she was when I saw her,
and just as able to bear her load of living
freight to its destination.
The diminished size and total loss of sight is in me,
not in her;

and just at the moment when someone at my side says,
'She is gone'
there are others who are watching her coming,
and other voices take up a glad shout –

'There she comes!'

– and that is dying.

BISHOP CHARLES H. BRENT

❤

'Often rebuked, yet always back returning'

Often rebuked, yet always back returning
   To those first feelings that were born with me,
And leaving busy chase of wealth and learning
   For idle dreams of things which cannot be:

Today, I will seek not the shadowy region;
   Its unsustaining vastness waxes drear;
And visions rising, legion after legion,
   Bring the unreal world too strangely near.

I'll walk, but not in old heroic traces,
   And not in paths of high morality,
And not among the half-distinguished faces,
   The clouded forms of long-past history.

I'll walk where my own nature would be leading:
   It vexes me to choose another guide:
Where the gray flocks in ferny glens are feeding;
   Where the wild wind blows on the mountain side.

What have those lonely mountains worth revealing?
   More glory and more grief than I can tell:
The earth that wakes *one* human heart to feeling
   Can centre both the worlds of Heaven and Hell.

EMILY BRONTË

❤

Rabbi Ben Ezra

I

Grow old along with me!
The best is yet to be,
The last of life, for which the first was made:
Our times are in His hand
Who saith 'A whole I planned,
Youth shows but half; trust God: see all nor be afraid!'

II

Not that, amassing flowers,
Youth sighed 'Which rose make ours,
Which lily leave and then as best recall?'
Not that, admiring stars,
It yearned 'Nor Jove, nor Mars;
Mine be some figured flame which blends, transcends them all!'

ROBERT BROWNING

She walks in beauty

She walks in beauty, like the night
Of cloudless climes and starry skies;
And all that's best of dark and bright
Meet in her aspect and her eyes:
Thus mellow'd to that tender light
Which heaven to gaudy day denies.

One shade the more, one ray the less,
Had half impair'd the nameless grace
Which waves in every raven tress,
Or softly lightens o'er her face;
Where thoughts serenely sweet express,
How pure, how dear their dwelling-place.

And on that cheek, and o'er that brow,
   So soft, so calm, yet eloquent,
The smiles that win, the tints that glow,
   But tell of days in goodness spent,
A mind at peace with all below,
   A heart whose love is innocent!

LORD BYRON

A valediction: forbidding mourning

As virtuous men passe mildly'away,
   And whisper to their soules, to goe,
Whilst some of their sad friends doe say,
   The breath goes now, and some say, no:

So let us melt, and make no noise,
   No teare-floods, nor sigh-tempests move,
'Twere prophanation of our joyes
   To tell the layetie our love.

Moving of th'earth brings harmes and feares,
   Men reckon what it did and meant,
But trepidation of the spheares
   Though greater farre, is innocent.

Dull sublunary lovers love
   (Whose soule is sense) cannot admit
Absence, because it doth remove
   Those things which elemented it.

But we by'a love, so much refin'd,
   That our selves know not what it is,
Inter-assured of the mind,
   Care less, eyes, lips, and hands to misse.

Our two soules therefore, which are one,
  Though I must goe, endure not yet
A breach, but an expansion,
  Like gold to ayery thinnesse beate.

If they be two, they are two so
  As stiffe twin compasses are two,
Thy soule the fixt foot, makes no show
  To move, but doth, if th'other doe.

And though it in the center sit,
  Yet when the other far doth rome,
It leanes, and hearkens after it,
  And growes erect, as it comes home.

Such wilt thou be to mee, who must
  Like th'other foot, obliquely runne;
Thy firmnes makes my circle just,
  And makes me end, where I begunne.

JOHN DONNE

Song

Sweetest love, I do not goe,
  For wearinesse of thee,
Nor in hope the world can show
  A fitter Love for mee;
    But since that I
Must dye at last, 'tis best,
To use my selfe in jest
    Thus by fain'd deaths to dye;

Yesternight the Sunne went hence,
  And yet is here to day,
He hath no desire nor sense,
  Nor halfe so short a way:

Then feare not mee,
But beleeve that I shall make
Speedier journeyes, since I take
    More wings and spurres then hee.

O how feeble is mans power,
    That if good fortune fall,
Cannot adde another houre,
    Nor a lost houre recall!
        But come bad chance,
And wee joyne to'it our strength,
And wee teach it art and length,
    It selfe o'r us to'advance.

When thou sigh'st, thou sigh'st not winde,
    But sigh'st my soule away,
When thou weep'st, unkindly kinde,
    My lifes blood doth decay.
        It cannot bee
That thou lov'st mee, as thou say'st,
If in thine my life thou waste,
    Thou art the best of mee.

Let not thy divining heart
    Forethinke me any ill,
Destiny may take thy part,
    And may thy feares fulfill;
        But thinke that wee
Are but turn'd aside to sleepe;
They who one another keepe
    Alive, ne'r parted bee.

JOHN DONNE

M—M—Memory

Scooping spilt, soft, broken oil
with a silver spoon
from a flagstone floor
into a clay bowl —

[37]

the dull scrape of the spoon
on the cool stone,
lukewarm drops in the bowl –

m–m–memory.

Kneel there,
words like fossils
trapped in the roof of the mouth,
forgotten, half-forgotten, half-
recalled, the tongue dreaming
it can trace their shape.

Names, ghosts, m–memory.

Through the high window of the hall
clouds obfuscate the sun
and you sit, exhaling grey smoke
into a purpling, religious light
trying to remember everything

perfectly
in time and space
where you cannot.

Those unstrung beads of oil
seem precious now, now
that the light has changed.

CAROL ANN DUFFY

❧

Extract from *LITTLE GIDDING, FOUR QUARTETS*

v

We shall not cease from exploration
And the end of all our exploring
Will be to arrive where we started
And know the place for the first time.

Through the unknown, remembered gate
When the last of earth left to discover
Is that which was the beginning;
At the source of the longest river
The voice of the hidden waterfall
And the children in the apple-tree
Not known, because not looked for
But heard, half-heard, in the stillness
Between two waves of the sea.
Quick now, here, now, always –
A condition of complete simplicity
(Costing not less than everything)
And all shall be well and
All manner of things shall be well
When the tongues of flames are in-folded
Into the crowned knot of fire
And the fire and the rose are one.

T.S. ELIOT

Extract from THE ROCK

x

We thank Thee for the lights that we have kindled,
The light of altar and of sanctuary;
Small lights of those who meditate at midnight
And lights directed through the coloured panes of windows
And light reflected from the polished stone,
The gilded carven wood, the coloured fresco.
Our gaze is submarine, our eyes look upward
And see the light that fractures through unquiet water.
We see the light but see not whence it comes.
O Light Invisible, we glorify Thee!

In our rhythm of earthly life we tire of light. We are glad when the day
    ends when the play ends; and ecstasy is too much pain.
We are children quickly tired: children who are up in the night and fall
    asleep as the rocket is fired; and the day is long for work or play.

We tire of distraction or concentration, we sleep and are glad to sleep,
Controlled by the rhythm of blood and the day and the night and the
  seasons.
And we must extinguish the candle, put out the light and relight it;
Forever must quench, forever relight the flame.

Therefore we thank Thee for our little light, that is dappled with shadow
We thank Thee who hast moved us to building, to finding, to forming a
  the ends of our fingers and beams of our eyes.
And when we have built an altar to the Invisible Light, we may set
  thereon the little lights for which our bodily vision is made.
And we thank Thee that darkness reminds us of light.
O Light Invisible, we give Thee thanks for Thy great glory!

T.S. ELIOT

Farewell my friends

It was beautiful
As long as it lasted
The journey of my life.

I have no regrets
Whatsoever save
The pain I'll leave behind.
Those dear hearts
Who love and care . . .
And the strings pulling
At the heart and soul . . .

The strong arms
That held me up
When my own strength
Let me down.

At every turning of my life
I came across
Good friends,
Friends who stood by me
Even when the time raced me by.

Farewell, farewell
My friends
I smile and
Bid you goodbye.
No, shed no tears
For I need them not
All I need is your smile.

If you feel sad
Do think of me
For that's what I'll like
When you live in the hearts
Of those you love
Remember then
You never die.

RABINDRANATH TAGORE

❧

'If I should go before the rest of you'

If I should go before the rest of you,
Break not a flower nor inscribe a stone.
Nor when I'm gone speak in a Sunday voice,
But be the usual selves that I have known.
Weep if you must,
Parting is hell,
But life goes on,
So sing as well.

JOYCE GRENFELL

❧

Love (III)

Love bade me welcome: yet my soul drew back,
        Guiltie of dust and sinne.
But quick-ey'd Love, observing me grow slack
        From my first entrance in,
Drew nearer to me, sweetly questioning,
        If I lack'd any thing.

[41]

A guest, I answer'd, worthy to be here:
    Love said, You shall be he.
I the unkinde, ungratefull? Ah my deare,
    I cannot look on thee.
Love took my hand, and smiling did reply,
    Who made the eyes but I?

Truth Lord, but I have marr'd them: let my shame
    Go where it doth deserve.
And know you not, sayes Love, who bore the blame?
    My deare, then I will serve.
You must sit down, sayes Love, and taste my meat:
    So I did sit and eat.

GEORGE HERBERT

Inversnaid

This darksome burn, horseback brown,
His rollrock highroad roaring down,
In coop and in comb the fleece of his foam
Flutes and low to the lake falls home.

A windpuff-bonnet of fawn-froth
Turns and twindles over the broth
Of a pool so pitchblack, fell-frowning,
It rounds and rounds Despair to drowning.

Degged with dew, dappled with dew
Are the groins of the braes that the brook treads through,
Wiry heathpacks, flitches of fern,
And the beadbonny ash that sits over the burn.

What would the world be, once bereft
Of wet and of wildness? Let them be left,
O let them be left, wildness and wet;
Long live the weeds and the wilderness yet.

GERARD MANLEY HOPKINS

More than an Elegy

What are you now then?
   A thought on the wind?
A balance of spirit and air?
   A released mind?

You are more, more than this
   Though sometimes seem less,
You are the pain death is
   And yet you bless.

Let me not intervene,
   Mark my shadow where
Only you now have been,
   Your spirit is there.

Where at best faith carries the heart.
   You are both air,
And earth and you are part
   Of a disciplined fire.

Let my missing you be
   What sometimes prayer
Is when it moves free.
Let me find you there.

But the daily truth is
   That I see most
In physical memories,
   You are never a ghost.

How curious love can be
   For now your death
Shows me how lovingly
   The voice finds breath.

The hands find useful things
   To do. O you are

The way a blackbird sings
And shapes the air.

ELIZABETH JENNINGS

Farewell

It is with hearts of sorrow and thoughts of joy
That we stand at this gunwale to say goodbye.
The water will cleanse you
The salt will heal you
The waves will cover you
I will never forget you.
The boat sails on to leave no trace
We're glad your soul has found a resting place.
Yet we know you haven't left us, for if we listen carefully
We can hear the rustle of your ballgown lace.

JONATHAN

If –

If you can keep your head when all about you
    Are losing theirs and blaming it on you,
If you can trust yourself when all men doubt you,
    But make allowance for their doubting too;
If you can wait and not be tired by waiting,
    Or being lied about, don't deal in lies,
Or being hated, don't give way to hating,
    And yet don't look too good, nor talk too wise:

If you can dream – and not make dreams your master;
    If you can think – and not make thoughts your aim;
If you can meet with Triumph and Disaster
    And treat those two impostors just the same;

If you can bear to hear the truth you've spoken
    Twisted by knaves to make a trap for fools,
Or watch the things you gave your life to, broken,
    And stoop and build 'em up with worn-out tools:

If you can make one heap of all your winnings
    And risk it on one turn of pitch-and-toss,
And lose, and start again at your beginnings
    And never breathe a word about your loss;
If you can force your heart and nerve and sinew
    To serve your turn long after they are gone,
And so hold on when there is nothing in you
    Except the Will which says to them: 'Hold on!'

If you can talk with crowds and keep your virtue,
    Or walk with Kings – nor lose the common touch,
If neither foes nor loving friends can hurt you,
    If all men count with you, but none too much;
If you can fill the unforgiving minute
    With sixty seconds' worth of distance run,
Yours is the Earth and everything that's in it,
    And – which is more – you'll be a Man, my son!

RUDYARD KIPLING

The long trail

There's a whisper down the field where the year has shot her yield,
    And the ricks stand grey to the sun,
Singing: 'Over then, come over, for the bee has quit the clover,
    'And your English summer's done.'

    You have heard the beat of the off-shore wind,
    And the thresh of the deep-sea rain;
    You have heard the song – how long? how long?
    Pull out on the trail again!
Ha' done with the Tents of Shem, dear lass,
We've seen the seasons through,
And it's time to turn on the old trail, our own trail, the out trail,
Pull out, pull out, on the Long Trail – the trail that is always new!

It's North you may run to the rime-ringed sun
  Or South to the blind Horn's hate;
Or East all the way into Mississippi Bay,
  Or West to the Golden Gate –
      Where the blindest bluffs hold good, dear lass,
      And the wildest tales are true,
      And the men bulk big on the old trail, our own trail, the out trail,
      And life runs large on the Long Trail – the trail that is always
        new.

The days are sick and cold, and the skies are grey and old,
  And the twice-breathed airs blow damp;
And I'd sell my tired soul for the bucking beam-sea roll
  Of a black Bilbao tramp,
      With her load-line over her hatch, dear lass,
      And a drunken Dago crew,
      And her nose held down on the old trail, our own trail, the out
        trail
      From Cadiz south on the Long Trail – the trail that is always
        new.

There be triple ways to take, of the eagle or the snake,
  Or the way of a man with a maid;
But the sweetest way to me is a ship's upon the sea
  In the heel of the North-East Trade.
      Can you hear the crash on her bows, dear lass,
      And the drum of the racing screw,
      As she ships it green on the old trail, our own trail, the out trail,
      As she lifts and 'scends on the Long Trail – the trail that is always
        new?

See the shaking funnels roar, with the Peter at the fore,
  And the fenders grind and heave,
And the derricks clack and grate, as the tackle hooks the crate,
  And the fall-rope whines through the sheave;
      It's 'Gang-plank up and in,' dear lass,
      It's 'Hawsers warp her through!'
      And it's 'All clear aft' on the old trail, our own trail, the out
        trail,
      We're backing down on the Long Trail – the trail that is always
        new.

O the mutter overside, when the port-fog holds us tied,
    And the sirens hoot their dread,
When foot by foot we creep o'er the hueless, viewless deep
    To the sob of the questing lead!
        It's down by the Lower Hope, dear lass,
        With the Gunfleet Sands in view,
        Till the Mouse swings green on the old trail, our own trail, the
          out trail,
        And the Gull Light lifts on the Long Trail – the trail that is
          always new.

O the blazing tropic night, when the wake's a welt of light
    That holds the hot sky tame,
And the steady fore-foot snores through the planet-powdered floors
    Where the scared whale flukes in flame!
        Her plates are flaked by the sun, dear lass,
        And her ropes are taut with the dew,
        For we're booming down on the old trail, our own trail, the
          out trail,
        We're sagging south on the Long Trail – the trail that is always
          new.

Then home, get her home, where the drunken rollers comb,
    And the shouting seas drive by,
And the engines stamp and ring, and the wet bows reel and swing,
    And the Southern Cross rides high!
        Yes, the old lost stars wheel back, dear lass,
        That blaze in the velvet blue.
        They're all old friends on the old trail, our own trail, the out
          trail,
        They're God's own guides on the Long Trail – the trail that is
          always new.

Fly forward, O my heart, from the Foreland to the Start –
    We're steaming all too slow,
And it's twenty thousand mile to our little lazy isle
    Where the trumpet-orchids blow!
        You have heard the call of the off-shore wind
        And the voice of the deep-sea rain;
        You have heard the song – how long? – how long?
        Pull out on the trail again!

The Lord knows what we may find, dear lass,
And The Deuce knows what we may do –
But we're back once more on the old trail, our own trail, the out trail,
We're down, hull-down, on the Long Trail – the trail that is always
    new!

RUDYARD KIPLING

from A CHARM

    Take of English earth as much
    As either hand may rightly clutch.
    In the taking of it breathe
    Prayer for all who lie beneath.
    Not the great nor well-bespoke,
    But the mere uncounted folk
    Of whose life and death is none
    Report or lamentation.
      Lay that earth upon thy heart,
      And thy sickness shall depart!

RUDYARD KIPLING

'Death stands above me'

Death stands above me, whispering low
    I know not what into my ear:
Of his strange language all I know
    Is, there is not a word of fear.

WALTER SAVAGE LANDOR

At grass

The eye can hardly pick them out
From the cold shade they shelter in,
Till wind distresses tail and mane;
Then one crops grass, and moves about
– The other seeming to look on –
And stands anonymous again.

Yet fifteen years ago, perhaps
Two dozen distances sufficed
To fable them: faint afternoons
Of Cups and Stakes and Handicaps,
Whereby their names were artificed
To inlay faded, classic Junes –

Silks at the start: against the sky
Numbers and parasols: outside,
Squadrons of empty cars, and heat,
And littered grass: then the long cry
Hanging unhushed till it subside
To stop-press columns on the street.

Do memories plague their ears like flies?
They shake their heads. Dusk brims the shadows.
Summer by summer all stole away,
The starting-gates, the crowds and cries –
All but the unmolesting meadows.
Almanacked, their names live; they

Have slipped their names, and stand at ease,
Or gallop for what must be joy,
And not a fieldglass sees them home,
Or curious stop-watch prophesies:
Only the groom, and the groom's boy,
With bridles in the evening come.

PHILIP LARKIN

Londonderry Air

I would be true, for there are those who trust me.
I would be pure, for there are those who care.
I would be strong, for there is much to suffer.
I would be brave, for there is much to dare.
I would be friend of all, the foe, the friendless.
I would be giving, and forget the gift.
I would be humble, for I know my weakness.
I would look up, and laugh and love and live.

ANON.

Jabberwocky

'Twas brillig, and the slithy toves
   Did gyre and gimble in the wabe:
All mimsy were the borogoves,
   And the mome raths outgrabe.

'Beware the Jabberwock, my son!
   The jaws that bite, the claws that catch!
Beware the Jubjub bird, and shun
   The frumious Bandersnatch!'

He took his vorpal sword in hand:
   Long time the manxome foe he sought –
So rested he by the Tumtum tree,
   And stood awhile in thought.

And, as in uffish thought he stood,
   The Jabberwock, with eyes of flame,
Came whiffling through the tulgy wood,
   And burbled as it came!

One, two! One, two! And through and through
   The vorpal blade went snicker-snack!
He left it dead, and with its head
   He went galumphing back.

'And hast thou slain the Jabberwock?
    Come to my arms, my beamish boy!
O frabjous day! Callooh! Callay!'
    He chortled in his joy.

'Twas brillig, and the slithy toves
    Did gyre and gimble in the wabe:
All mimsy were the borogoves,
    And the mome raths outgrabe.

LEWIS CARROLL

Pegasus

(IN MEMORIAM: L. B. L.)★

It was there on the hillside, no tall traveller's story.
A cloud caught on a whin-bush, an airing of bleached
Linen, a swan, the cliff of a marble quarry –
It could have been any of these: but as he approached,
He saw that it was indeed what he had cause
Both to doubt and believe in – a horse, a winged white horse.

It filled the pasture with essence of solitude.
The wind tiptoed away like an interloper,
The sunlight there became a transparent hood
Estranging what it revealed; and the bold horse-coper,
The invincible hero, trudging up Helicon,
Knew he had never before been truly alone.

It stood there, solid as ivory, dreamy as smoke;
Or moved, and its hooves went dewdropping so lightly
That even the wild cyclamen were not broken:
But when those hooves struck rock, such was their might
They tapped a crystal vein which flowed into song
As it ran through thyme and grasses down-along.

★ L.B.L. was the poet Lilian Bowes Lyon.

'Pegasus,' he called, 'Pegasus' – with the surprise
Of one for the first time naming his naked lover.
The creature turned its lordly, incurious eyes
Upon the young man; but they seemed to pass him over
As something beneath their pride or beyond their ken.
It returned to cropping the violets and cyclamen.

CECIL DAY LEWIS

Testament

'But how can I live without you?' she cried.

I left all the world to you and when I died;
Beauty of earth and air and sea;
Leap of a swallow or a tree;
Kiss of rain and wind's embrace;
Passion of storm and winter's face;
Touch of feather, flower and stone;
Chiselled line of branch or bone;
Flight of stars, night's caravan;
Song of crickets – and of man –
All these I put in my testament,
All these I bequeathed you when I went.

'But how can I see them without your eyes
Or touch them without your hand?
How can I hear them without your ear,
Without your heart, understand?'

These too, these too, I leave to you!

ANNE MORROW LINDBERGH

Compassionate crusader – for Bill

She said 'You must die smiling –
With a smile on your face'
What about living?
Living too must be with a smile.
An 'inner' smile. Content.
Not accepting – necessarily –
But knowing your role.
Fulfilling your dream.

That dream can be a crusade
A cry from the heart
A railing against abuse of innocence.
There is contentment in that.

Knowing your arrow speeds to the target
True to your self – your inner thoughts –
Not to kill the enemy
But piercing him with shafts of light.
Little wounds that strip away pretence
Tearing away the mask.

In the end the tangible is no more
We are dust in the wind.
But spirits whisper, echo in the air
And enter into unsuspecting dreams.

When my old soul is spinning in the sky
My darts will never let those others sleep –
Spur them to questioning –
Wanting doubt to seed those shuttered minds.

If only I can prick that round balloon
That little blinded empire
Then I will die smiling.
Be content.

VIRGINIA MCKENNA

Ode

We are the music-makers,
    And we are the dreamers of dreams,
Wandering by lone sea-breakers,
    And sitting by desolate streams;
World-losers and world-forsakers,
    On whom the pale moon gleams:
Yet we are the movers and shakers
    Of the world for ever, it seems.

With wonderful deathless ditties
We build up the world's great cities,
    And out of a fabulous story
    We fashion an empire's glory:
One man with a dream, at pleasure,
    Shall go forth and conquer a crown;
And three with a new song's measure
    Can trample an empire down.

We, in the ages lying
    In the buried past of the earth,
Built Nineveh with our sighing,
    And Babel itself with our mirth;
And o'erthrew them with prophesying
    To the old of the new world's worth;
For each age is a dream that is dying,
    Or one that is coming to birth.

ARTHUR WILLIAM EDGAR O'SHAUGHNESSY

One perfect rose

A single flow'r he sent me, since we met.
    All tenderly his messenger he chose;
Deep-hearted, pure, with scented dew still wet –
    One perfect rose.

I knew the language of the floweret;
   'My fragile leaves,' it said, 'his heart enclose.'
Love long has taken for his amulet
   One perfect rose.

Why is it no one ever sent me yet
   One perfect limousine, do you suppose?
Ah no, it's always just my luck to get
   One perfect rose.

DOROTHY PARKER

'They that love beyond the world'

They that love beyond the world, cannot be separated by it.
Death cannot kill what never dies.
Nor can spirits ever be divided that love and live in the same divine
   principle, the root and record of their friendship.
If absence be not death, neither is theirs.
Death is but crossing the world, as friends do the seas; they live in one
   another still.
For they must needs be present, that love and live in that which is
   omnipresent.
This is the comfort of friends, that though they may be said to die, yet
   their friendship and society are ever present, because immortal.

WILLIAM PENN

Song

When I am dead, my dearest,
sing no sad songs for me;
Plant thou no roses at my head,
Nor shady cypress tree:

Be the green grass above me
With showers and dewdrops wet:
And if thou wilt, remember,
And if thou wilt, forget.
I shall not see the shadows,
I shall not feel the rain;
I shall not hear the nightingale
sing on as if in pain:
And dreaming through the twilight
That doth not rise nor set,
Haply I may remember,
And haply may forget.

CHRISTINA GEORGINA ROSSETTI

from HENRY V

I pray thee, bear my former answer back:
Bid them achieve me and then sell my bones.
Good God! Why should they mock poor fellows thus?
The man that once did sell the lion's skin
While the beast liv'd, was kill'd with hunting him.
A many of our bodies shall no doubt
find native graves; upon the which, I trust,
Shall witness live in brass of this day's work;
And those that leave their valiant bones in France,
Dying like men, though buried in your dunghills,
They shall be fam'd; for there the sun shall greet them,
And draw their honours reeking up to heaven,
Leaving their earthly parts to choke your clime,
The smell whereof shall breed a plague in France.
Mark then abounding valour in our English,
That being dead, like to the bullet's grazing,
Break out into a second course of mischief,
Killing in relapse of mortality.
Let me speak proudly: tell the constable,
We are but warriors for the working-day;

Our gayness and our gilt are all besmirch'd
With rainy marching in the painful field;
There's not a piece of feather in our host –
Good argument, I hope, we will not fly –
And time hath worn us into slovenry:
But, by the mass, our hearts are in the trim;
And my poor soldiers tell me, yet ere night
They'll be in fresher robes, or they will pluck
The gay new coats o'er the French soldiers' heads,
And turn them out of service. If they do this, –
As, if God please, they shall – my ransom then
Will soon be levied. Herald, save though thy labour;
Come thou no more for ransom, gentle herald:
They shall have none, I swear, but these my joints;
Which if they have as I will leave 'em them,
Shall yield them little, tell the constable.

WILLIAM SHAKESPEARE

Sonnet 71

No longer mourn for me when I am dead,
Then you shall hear the surly sullen bell
Give warning to the world that I am fled
From this vile world with vilest worms to dwell:
Nay if you read this line, remember not,
The hand that writ it, for I love you so,
That I in your sweet thoughts would be forgot,
If thinking on me then should make you woe.
O if (I say) you look upon this verse,
When I (perhaps) compounded am with clay,
Do not so much as my poor name rehearse;
But let your love even with my life decay.
    Lest the wise world should look into your mone,
    And mock you with me after I am gone.

WILLIAM SHAKESPEARE

Sonnet 116

Let me not to the marriage of true minds
Admit impediments; love is not love
Which alters when it alteration finds,
Or bends with the remover to remove.
O no, it is an ever-fixèd mark
That looks on tempests and is never shaken;
It is the star to every wandering bark,
Whose worth's unknown although his height be taken.
Love's not Time's fool, though rosy lips and cheeks
Within his bending sickle's compass come;
Love alters not with his brief hours and weeks,
But bears it out even to the edge of doom.
   If this be error and upon me proved,
   I never writ, nor no man ever loved.

WILLIAM SHAKESPEARE

'To his friend in absence'

When the moon's splendour shines in naked heaven,
   Stand thou and gaze beneath the open sky.
See how that radiance from her lamp is riven,
   And in one splendour foldeth gloriously
Two that have loved, and now divided far,
Bound by love's bond, in heart together are.

What though thy lover's eyes in vain desire thee,
   Seek for love's face, and find that face denied?
Let that light be between us for a token;
   Take this poor verse that love and faith inscribe.
Love, art thou true? and fast love's chain about thee?
Then for all time, O love, God give thee joy!

WALAFRID STRABO
Translated by Helen Waddell

'And death shall have no dominion'

And death shall have no dominion.
Dead men naked they shall be one
With the man in the wind and the west moon;
When their bones are picked clean and the clean bones gone,
They shall have stars at elbow and foot;
Though they go mad they shall be sane,
Though they sink through the sea they shall rise again;
Though lovers be lost love shall not;
And death shall have no dominion.

And death shall have no dominion.
Under the windings of the sea
They lying long shall not die windily;
Twisting on racks when sinews give way,
Strapped to a wheel, yet they shall not break;
Faith in their hands shall snap in two,
And the unicorn evils run them through;
Split all ends up they shan't crack;
And death shall have no dominion.

And death shall have no dominion.
No more may gulls cry at their ears
Or waves break loud on the seashores;
Where blew a flower may a flower no more
Lift its head to the blows of the rain;
Though they be made and dead as nails,
Heads of the characters hammer through daisies;
Break in the sun till the sun breaks down,
And death shall have no dominion.

DYLAN THOMAS

Lights out

I have come to the borders of sleep,
The unfathomable deep
Forest where all must lose
Their way, however straight,
Or winding, soon or late;
They cannot choose.

Many a road and track
That, since the dawn's first crack,
Up to the forest brink,
Deceived the travellers,
Suddenly now blurs,
And in they sink.

Here love ends,
Despair, ambition ends;
All pleasure and all trouble,
Although most sweet or bitter,
Here ends in sleep that is sweeter
Than tasks most noble.

There is not any book
Or face of dearest look
That I would not turn from now
To go into the unknown
I must enter, and leave, alone,
I know not how.

The tall forest towers;
Its cloudy foliage lowers
Ahead, shelf above shelf;
Its silence I hear and obey
That I may lose my way
And myself.

EDWARD THOMAS

from THANKSGIVINGS FOR THE BODY

O what praises are due unto Thee,
  Who hast made me
    A living inhabitant
      Of the great world.
    And the centre of it!
  A sphere of sense,
     And a mine of riches,
Which when bodies are dissected fly away.
  The spacious room
    Which Thou hast hidden in mine eye,
  The chambers for sounds
    Which Thou hast prepar'd in mine ear,
  The receptacles for smells
    Concealed in my nose;
  The feeling of my hands,
    The taste of my tongue.
But above all, O Lord, the glory of speech, whereby Thy servant is
enabled with praise to celebrate Thee.
       For
All the beauties in Heaven and earth,
The melody of sounds,
The sweet odours
    Of Thy dwelling-place.
The delectable pleasures that gratify my sense,
    That gratify the feeling of mankind.
The light of history,
    Admitted by the ear.
The light of Heaven,
    Brought in by the eye.
The volubility and liberty
    Of my hands and members.
Fitted by Thee for all operations;
    Which the fancy can imagine,
      Or soul desire:
From the framing of a needle's eye,
  To the building of a tower:
From the squaring of trees,
    To the polishing of kings' crowns.

For all the mysteries, engines, instruments, wherewith the world is filled, which we are able to frame and use to Thy glory.
For all the trades, variety of operations, cities, temples, streets, bridges, mariner's compass, admirable picture, sculpture, writing, printing, songs and music, wherewith the world is beautified and adorned.

THOMAS TRAHERNE

Gaudeamus igitur

Come, no more of grief and dying!
Sing the time too swiftly flying.
    Just an hour
    Youth's in flower,
Give me roses to remember
In the shadow of December.

    Give me music, give me rapture,
Youth that's fled none can recapture;
    Not with thought,
    Wisdom's bought.
Out on pride and scorn and sadness!
Give me laughter, give me gladness.

Sweetest Earth, I love and love thee,
Seas about thee, skies above thee,
    Suns and storms,
    Hues and forms
Of the clouds with fleeting shadows
One thy mountains and thy meadows.

    When at last the grasses cover
Me, the world's unwearied lover,
    If regret
    Haunt me yet,
It shall be for joys untasted,
Nature lent and folly wasted.

Youth and jests and summer weather,
Goods that kings and clowns together
    Waste or use
    As they choose,
These, the best, we miss pursuing
Sullen shades that mock our wooing.

Feigning age will not delay it —
When the reckoning comes we'll pay it,
    Our own mirth
    Has been worth
All the forfeit, light or heavy
Wintry Time and Fortune levy.

Feigning grief will not escape it,
What though ne'er so well you ape it —
    Age and care
    All must share,
All alike must pay hereafter,
Some for tears and some for laughter.

Know, ye sons of Melancholy,
To be wise and young is folly.
    Tis the weak
    Fear to wreak
On this clay of life their fancies,
Shaping battles, shaping dances.

While ye scorn our names unspoken,
Roses dead and garlands broken,
    O ye wise,
    We arise,
Out of failures, dreams, disasters,
We arise to be your masters.

MARGARET L. WOODS

I don't believe in death

I don't believe in death
Who comes in silent stealth
He robs us only of a breath
Not of a lifetime's wealth

I don't believe the tomb
Imprisons us in earth
It's but another loving womb
Preparing our new birth

I do believe in life
Empowered from above
Till, freed from stress and worldly strife
We soar through realms above

I do believe that then
In joy that never ends
We'll meet all those we've loved, again
And celebrate our friends.

PAULINE WEBB

Readings

from FACTS OF THE FAITH

A last message from the one we loved is: 'Death is nothing at all. It does not count. I have only slipped away into the next room. Nothing has happened. Everything remains exactly as it was. I am I, and you are you, and the old life that we lived so fondly together is untouched, unchanged. Whatever we were to each other, that we are still. Call me by the old familiar name. Speak of me in the easy way which you always used. Put no difference into your tone. Wear no forced air of solemnity or sorrow. Laugh as we always laughed at the little jokes that we enjoyed together. Play, smile, think of me, pray for me. Let my name be ever the household word that it always was. Life means all that it ever meant. It is the same as it ever was. There is absolute and unbroken continuity. What is this death but a negligible accident? Why should I be out of mind because I am out of sight? I am waiting for you, for an interval, somewhere very near, just round the corner. All is well. Nothing is hurt; nothing is lost. One brief moment and all will be as it was before. How we shall laugh at the trouble of parting when we meet again!'

HENRY SCOTT HOLLAND

BILL CARTER TAKES OVER

NARRATOR: An eschatological comedy in five acts, set in the future but based on the *Book of Revelation*.

Act I: God Experiences the Miracle of Pain
It is dawn over England on a winter Wednesday. The clocks have gone back but privatization of everything else has gone forward.

In Number 12 Thatcher Tenements, Bill Carter gets up before the rest of his little family.

Carter switches on the kettle for a mug of tea and goes into the living-room to have a look at God.

CARTER: Not much of a day, O Lord.

NARRATOR: God was used to criticism and said nothing. He curled a flipper and made another circuit of His tank. God's tank was the standard size, just under 2 metres square on its base, and 1.4 metres high. Its top was open to the air. It contained nothing but air and God.

CARTER: I don't think Judy's flu is any better this morning, Lord. I can hear her sneezing in her room. Can't You do something about that? You know her exams are coming up.

NARRATOR: 'I do have your daughter's interests in mind,' God spake.

CARTER: You know I don't complain, O Lord, but please let today be something special.

NARRATOR: God's single eye was rather like a peony. Its petals opened; among the dense stamens something glittered. When God manifested Himself to a troubled world in the closing years of the twentieth century, He chose to appear universally in this non-anthropomorphic form. Those people who were against racism applauded this; those people who were for it thought God was being silly.

GOD: All is well, Carter. All is eternally well. Time does not really pass, you know. You live with Me in an Eternal day.

CARTER: Christ, you always fob me off with words, Lord! I was only worried about Judy's flu.

GOD: I'm only here as a witness to My presence in the universe. I really prefer not to work little local miracles, having found from experience that they're counter-productive.

CARTER: But You're omnipotent, *omnipotent*! You made the damned galaxies! Don't give me that counter-productive nonsense.

GOD: You will have to accept that even omnipotence has its limits.

CARTER: Oh, come on, will you, God? Look, You know the mess my life is in. I've got another session with Mrs Batacharya this evening. Help me, will You? I ask you every day –

GOD: And every day I do help you, Bill, in many ways . . .

NARRATOR: In sudden rage, Carter heaved himself into the big glass tank. God writhed away to the far side, but Carter grasped one of His trailing flippers and got in a swift kick at one of the three segments of His body.

GOD: Ow! That hurts! You know We can't stand pain!

CARTER: That's ridiculous –

GOD: How else could We comprehend mankind's problems if We felt no pain? Owww!

NARRATOR: Throwing himself forward, Carter locked both hands round the smooth neck-like stalk connecting first and second segments. He had God pinned down on one side of the tank, in a fairly undignified position.

CARTER: Now, look! I want a miracle out of You, then I'll let go. Quick!

GOD: Owww . . . What do you want Me to do?

CARTER: You can do anything, *anything*, and You ask me what I want? How about a bigger house, on a hill somewhere, beautiful views, with a stream – a trout stream –, and a pretty wife. With a lake and a power-boat on it. Two wives. Sisters, who get on well together. Good dress sense. A full-size statue of Tina Turner in the hall. And a good job. No, no work, just the estate to look after. I want to be a crack shot, really crack. A private armoury. Wild elephants in the grounds, really danger-ous. Servants. Drink. Women. Fame. A modem. You know what I want. Make them materialize and I'll let You go.

GOD: Yes, I do know what you want, Carter, and believe Me I sympa-thize, deeply. Owww! Steady on . . . All those things, those gross mate-rial things, would really be only a substitute for a state of spiritual – Owww! Mercy!

CARTER: One small miracle, come on, or I'm keeping You pinned down here all day, O Lord. Anything! How about a palm tree in the back garden?

GOD: The neighbours would complain. Ohhh, Jesus, Carter, you have a nasty streak in you . . .

CARTER: Who put it there? Come on, a palm tree or I'll tear this flipper thing right off!

NARRATOR: Over the garden, a flash of lightning. By Laura's rockery, a palm tree grew, its topknot of leaves blotting out the chimneys of the houses opposite.

As Carter climbed out of the tank, victorious but unsatisfied, God relapsed sulkily into a corner. He was sick of doing palm trees.

Act II: God Experiences the Old Folks' Home

NARRATOR: After breakfast, Carter drove to see his elderly mother in her old folks' home, round in Profumo Place. She was eighty-one, her skin blotched by liver-marks as if by a poisonous fungus.

The old woman explained to Carter what a rotten night she had had, looking pointedly at God as she did so.

God drifted in His glass tank in one corner of the room, behind the commode, by the oxygen cylinder.

MOTHER: It's Mrs Walker, she's stone deaf. You should have heard her at two this morning. Disgraceful! Poor thing. No consideration. I'm trying to get them to move her. God, God, why You don't help me I don't know! Nobody cares for a poor old woman any more.

GOD: I care. That's why I'm here, suffering with you. Be patient, my dear. All's well. All is eternally well.

MOTHER: That's a lot of help, I'm sure.

CARTER: I'd better be getting to work, Mother.

MOTHER: You don't stay long, do you?

CARTER: You've got God to communicate with, bear that in mind.

MOTHER: Oh, *He*'s no company. He keeps going on about the Hereafter.

GOD: That's untrue, Mrs Carter. I read you a whole Barbara Cartland romance yesterday. But, as I told you then, the Hereafter represents a happier state.

MOTHER: There He goes again, you see?

CARTER: (*stands*) At least He loves us all. Bye, mother.

Act III: God Remembers Top of the Pops

NARRATOR: That evening, for once, the after-work traffic jams were not so bad. He was home by half-past five. As Carter stood in the hall removing his coat, Laura came downstairs, smiling. She put her arms round him.

LAURA: Have some tea. Come in the kitchen and talk to me.

NARRATOR: They perched on stools at the kitchen bar facing one another as the kettle boiled. Her God's tank was wedged in the space between the oven and the fridge.

CARTER: On the way home, they were playing 'Eso Beso'. (*He hums a few bars.*) Do you remember that one, darling, when we were kids?

LAURA: Who was it used to sing 'Eso Beso'?

CARTER: I've forgotten – it's so long ago.

GOD: It was Paul Anka.

LAURA: Those sixties songs had more zip than the stuff they pour out now. The nineties are a bit of a flop, aren't they? Perhaps next century will be better. But that's up to You, O Lord Almighty?

GOD: No, it's up to you and your husband and everyone else, my dear. I can only work through you, as you strive for a better world.

LAURA: Crikey, me strive for a better world? It's all I can do to hold my marriage together. I'm not appreciated, that's the trouble. Work morning, noon, and night . . . Without being unpleasant, God, I think You created a lot of unfairness between the sexes.

CARTER: I wonder what happened to Paul Anka.

GOD: Bill, it's 6.10, time you went to your marriage guidance counsellor.

LAURA: Oh, you're going to tittle-tattle to that woman again.

CARTER: Why don't you come with me, dear?

LAURA: I've got other things to do with my time. You ought to jog round the park like Paul Gutteridge does. Much better for you than going to that awful Batacharya woman every Wednesday evening.

CARTER: Look, please behave yourself while I'm away.
LAURA: And what is that supposed to mean?
CARTER: Just remember God is watching you.

Act IV: God experiences Psychotherapy

NARRATOR: He was early at the Clinic. The habit of punctuality was hard to shake, even though Mrs Batacharya had once uttered a deadly insult and called him 'anally-oriented'. Mrs Batacharya wore a sari with a cardigan over it, and embroidered slippers. She kept God behind a fabric screen.
BATACHARYA: How have you been, Bill?
CARTER: Bunty, I believe that my wife is continuing her affair with that bastard, Gutteridge. I don't know whether I'm imagining it or not. What's imagination, what's reality? God's presence hasn't made the distinction between them easier to grasp.
GOD: Both are aspects of My Eternal Being.
BATACHARYA: Ignore Him. He has been very loquacious today. Just concentrate on me. How has the week been, Bill?
CARTER: I beat up God this morning until He produced a palm tree – I suppose that's on my conscience.
BATACHARYA: One measly palm tree?
GOD: It was a *cocos nucifera*, to remind Carter of how such trees dump thousands of tons of fruit daily into the ungrateful laps of mankind.
BATACHARYA: You're always preaching, O Lord. Take it from me, it's counter-productive.
CARTER: Outside, in the real world, people know for sure whether their wives love them or not.
BATACHARYA: And in that real world, does Laura know if her Bill loves her?
CARTER: . . . I tell her often enough. Don't I, God?
GOD: Love lives in deeds as well as words. When I created the world, that was a deed of love, and you are all the children of it. You would save yourselves endless sorrow if you could remember that cardinal fact.
BATACHARYA: Bill's trouble is that, as well as Laura and himself, You also created Gutteridge.

Act V: God experiences God

NARRATOR: Carter downed a couple of beers before he drove home from the clinic. His wife was absent. No food had been prepared. There was nothing in the fridge.

After a moment's hesitation, Carter went into the dining-room to see his own incarnation of God. Closing the door and leaning against it, he looked at the Being who moved languidly in His tank.

CARTER: Well, Wednesday's almost over, and it didn't have much to offer. I'm sorry I hurt You this morning, by the way: that was a really disgusting performance.

GOD: I'm touched by your penitence, but you should learn to control yourself.

CARTER: Isn't that part of Your job? You made us, after all.

GOD: You see, that's what makes Me so absolutely fed up. You humans winge and whine for autonomy. You get it. Then when anything goes wrong you blame Me. How do you think I feel? Grow up, will you?

CARTER: So what about Judy then? Is she going to be fit to go to school tomorrow, or not?

GOD: I'm the *Creator*, Carter, not your family doctor.

CARTER: Surely You must be fed up in there, not getting through to humanity, just performing a minor conjuring trick now and again. Why don't You try a really major miracle for once? It might improve Your morale as well as everyone else's.

GOD: What do you suggest?

CARTER: You see, You've no imagination . . .

GOD: So what do you suggest?

CARTER: . . . I wish I had Your job!

NARRATOR: Next moment, Hallelujah! He found himself dispersed among a myriad tanks, staring out at the whole of humanity. In the background, joy, trumpets, and the thrilling tintinnabulations of galaxies.

Countless representatives of humanity stared back at him, aware that something inexplicable had happened. For once, everyone's attention was centred on God.

And God spake.

CARTER (*after a pause*): All is well. And all is eternally well.

NARRATOR: What else could he have told them?

BRIAN W. ALDISS

from LUCKY JIM

Dixon was alive again. Consciousness was upon him before he could get out of the way; not for him the slow, gracious wandering from the halls of sleep, but a summary, forcible ejection. He lay sprawled, too wicked to move, spewed up like a broken spider-crab on the tarry shingle of the morning. The light did him harm, but not as much as looking at things did; he resolved, having done it once, never to move his eye-balls again. A dusty thudding in his head made the scene before him beat like a pulse. His mouth had been used as a latrine by some small creature of the night, and then as its mausoleum. During the night, too, he'd somehow been on a cross-country run and then been expertly beaten up by secret police. He felt bad.

He reached out for and put on his glasses. At once he saw that something was wrong with the bedclothes immediately before his face. Endangering his chance of survival, he sat up a little, and what met his bursting eyes roused to a frenzy the timpanist in his head. A large, irregular area of the turned-back part of the sheet was missing; a smaller but still considerable area of the turned-back part of the blanket was missing; an area about the size of the palm of his hand in the main part of the top blanket was missing. Through the three holes, which, ap-propriately enough, had black borders, he could see a dark brown mark on the second blanket. He ran a finger round a bit of the hole in the sheet, and when he looked at his finger it bore a dark-grey stain. That meant ash; ash meant burning; burning must mean cigarettes. Had this cigarette burnt itself out on the blanket? If not, where was it now? Nowhere on the bed; nor in it. He leaned over the side, gritting his teeth; a sunken brown channel, ending in a fragment of discoloured paper, lay across a light patch in the pattern of a valuable-looking rug. This made him feel very unhappy, a feeling sensibly increased when he looked at the bedside table. This was marked by two black, charred grooves, greyish and shiny in parts, lying at right angles and stopping well short of the ashtray, which held a single used match. On the table were two unused matches; the remainder lay with the empty cigarette packet on the floor. The bakelite mug was nowhere to be seen.

Had he done all this himself? Or had a wayfarer, a burglar, camped out in his room? Or was he the victim of some Horla fond of tobacco? He thought that on the whole he must have done it himself, and wished he hadn't.

KINGSLEY AMIS

from THE PROPHET

Then Almitra spoke, saying, We would ask now of death.
And he said:
You would know the secret of death.
But how shall you find it unless you seek it in the heart of life?
The owl whose night-bound eyes are blind unto the day cannot unveil the mystery of light.

If you would indeed behold the spirit of death, open your heart wide unto the body of life.

For life and death are one, even as the river and the sea are one.

In the depth of your hopes and desires lies your silent knowledge of the beyond;

And like seeds dreaming beneath the snow your heart dreams of spring.

Trust the dreams, for in them is hidden the gate to eternity.

Your fear of death is but the trembling of the shepherd when he stands before the king whose hand is to be laid upon him in honour.

Is the shepherd not joyful beneath his trembling, that he shall wear the mark of the King?

Yet is he not more mindful of his trembling?

For what is it to die but to stand naked in the wind and to melt into the sun?

And what is it to cease breathing but to free the breath from its restless tides, that it may rise and expand and seek God unencumbered?

Only when you drink from the river of silence shall you indeed sing.

And when you have reached the mountain top, then you shall begin to climb.

And when the earth shall claim your limbs, then shall you truly dance.

KAHLIL GIBRAN

from PRIDE AND PREJUDICE

It is a truth universally acknowledged, that a single man in possession of a good fortune must be in want of a wife. However little known the feelings or views of such a man may be on his first entering a neighbourhood, this truth is so well fixed in the minds of the surrounding families, that he is considered as the rightful property of some one or other of their daughters.

'My dear Mr Bennet,' said his lady to him one day, 'have you heard that Netherfield Park is let at last?'

Mr Bennet replied that he had not.

'But it is,' returned she; 'for Mrs Long has just been here and she told me all about it.'

Mr Bennet made no answer.

'Do not you want to know who has taken it?' cried his wife impatiently.

'*You* want to tell me and I have no objection to hearing it.'

This was invitation enough.

'Why, my dear, you must know, Mrs Long says that Netherfield is taken by a young man of large fortune from the north of England; that he came down on Monday in a chaise and four to see the place, and was so much delighted with it, that he agreed with Mr Morris immediately; that he is to take possession before Michaelmas, and some of his servants are to be in the house by the end of next week.'

'What is his name?'

'Bingley.'

'Is he married or single?'

'Oh! single, my dear, to be sure! A single man of large fortune; four or five thousand a-year. What a fine thing for our girls!'

'How so! how can it affect them?'

'My dear Mr Bennet,' replied his wife, 'how can you be so tiresome! you must know that I am thinking of his marrying one of them.'

'Is that his design in settling here?'

'Design! nonsense, how can you talk so! But it is very likely that he *may* fall in love with one of them, and therefore you must visit him as soon as he comes.'

'I see no occasion for that. You and the girls may go, or you may send them by themselves, which perhaps will be still better, for as you are as handsome as any of them, Mr Bingley might like you the best of the party.'

'My dear, you flatter me. I certainly *have* had my share of beauty, but I do not pretend to be anything extraordinary now. When a woman has five grown-up daughters, she ought to give over thinking of her own beauty.'

'In such cases, a woman has not often much beauty to think of.'

'But, my dear, you must indeed go and see Mr Bingley when he comes into the neighbourhood.'

'It is more than I engage for, I assure you.'

'But consider your daughters. Only think what an establishment it would be for one of them. Sir William and Lady Lucas are determined to go, merely on that account, for in general, you know, they visit no newcomers. Indeed you must go, for it will be impossible for *us* to visit him if you do not.'

'You are over-scrupulous, surely. I dare say Mr Bingley will be very glad to see you; and I will send a few lines by you to assure him of my hearty consent to his marrying whichever he chooses of the girls; though I must throw in a good word for my little Lizzy.'

'I desire you will do no such thing. Lizzy is not a bit better than the others; and I am sure she is not half so handsome as Jane, nor half so good-humoured as Lydia. But you are always giving *her* the preference.'

'They have none of them much to recommend them,' replied he; 'they are all silly and ignorant, like other girls; but Lizzy has something more of quickness than her sisters.'

'Mr Bennet, how can you abuse your own children in such a way! You take delight in vexing me. You have no compassion on my poor nerves.'

'You mistake me, my dear. I have a high respect for your nerves. They are my old friends. I have heard you mention them with consideration these twenty years at least.'

'Ah! you do not know what I suffer.'

JANE AUSTEN

LETTER IN ACKNOWLEDGEMENT OF WEDDING PRESENT

DEAR LADY AMBLESHAM,

Who gives quickly, says the old proverb, gives twice. For this reason I have purposely delayed writing to you, lest I should appear to thank you more than once for the small, cheap, hideous present you sent me on the occasion of my recent wedding. Were you a poor woman, that little bowl of ill-imitated Dresden china would convict you of tastelessness merely; were you a blind woman, of nothing but an odious parsimony. As you have normal eyesight and more than usual wealth, your gift to me proclaims you at once a Philistine and a miser (or rather did so proclaim you until, less than ten seconds after I had unpacked it from its wrappings of tissue paper, I took it to the open window and had the satisfaction of seeing it shattered to atoms on the pavement). But stay! I perceive a possible flaw in my argument. Perhaps you were guided in your choice by a definite wish to insult me. I am sure, on reflection, that this was so. *I shall not forget.*

Yours, etc.,

CYNTHIA BEAUMARSH.

PS.   My husband asks me to tell you to warn Lord Amblesham to keep out of his way or to assume some disguise so complete that he will not be recognised by him and horsewhipped.

PPS.   I am sending copies of this letter to the principal London and provincial newspapers.

MAX BEERBOHM

from A LETTER TO A FRIEND, UPON OCCASION OF THE DEATH OF HIS INTIMATE FRIEND

Death hath not only particular Stars in Heaven, but malevolent Places on Earth, which single out our Infirmities, and strike at our weaker Parts; in which Concern, passager and migrant Birds have the great Advantages; who are naturally constituted for distant habitations, whom no Seas nor Places limit, but in their appointed Seasons will visit us from *Greenland* and Mount *Atlas*, and as some think, even from the *Antipodes*.

   Tho we could not have his Life, yet we missed not our desires in his soft Departure, which was scarce an Expiration; and his End not unlike his Beginning, when the salient Point scarce affords a sensible motion, and his Departure so like unto Sleep, that he scarce needed the civil Ceremony of closing his Eyes; contrary unto the common way wherein Death draws up, Sleep lets fall the Eye-lids. With what strift and pains we came into the World we know not; but 'tis commonly no easie matter to get out of it . . .

THOMAS BROWNE

from HYMN OF THE UNIVERSE

HUMANITY IN PROGRESS: PENSÉE 20

The world is a-building. This is the basic truth which must first be understood so thoroughly that it becomes an habitual and as it were natural springboard for our thinking. At first sight, beings and their destinies might seem to us to be scattered haphazard or at least in an arbitrary fashion over the face of the earth; we could very easily suppose that each of us might *equally well* have been born earlier or later, at this place or that, happier or more ill-starred, as though the universe from the beginning to end of its history formed in space-time a sort of vast flower-bed in which the flowers could be changed about at the whim of the gardener. But this idea is surely untenable. The more one reflects, with the help of all that science, philosophy and religion can teach us, each in its own field, the more one comes to realize that the world should be likened not to a bundle of elements artificially held together but rather to some organic system animated by a broad movement of development which is proper to itself. As the centuries go by it seems that a comprehensive plan is indeed being slowly carried out around us. A process is at work in the universe, an issue is at stake, which can best be compared to the processes of gestation and birth; the birth of that spiritual reality which is formed by souls and by such material reality as their existence involves. Laboriously, through and thanks to the activity of mankind, the new earth is being formed and purified and is taking on definition and clarity. No, we are not like the cut flowers that make up a bouquet: we are like the leaves and buds of a great tree on which everything appears at its proper time and place as required and determined by the good of the whole.

PIERRE TEILHARD DE CHARDIN

'They shall awake'

They shall awake as Jacob did, and say as Jacob said, Surely the Lord is in this place, and this is no other but the house of God, and the gate of heaven, And into that gate they shall enter, and in that house they shall dwell, where there shall be no Cloud nor Sun, no darkness nor dazzling, but one equal light, no noise nor silence, but one equal music, no fears nor hopes, but one equal possession, no foes nor friends, but one equal communion and Identity, no ends nor beginnings, but one equal eternity.

JOHN DONNE

from MEMORIALS: An Anthology of Poetry and Prose

. . . I am increasingly sure that life is spiritual and therefore continuous – not in the spiritualistic way (material) but as the actual fact of our being, and because I believe this I'm sure that prayer which says 'Death is an horizon and our horizon is but the limitation of our view' is the truth.

We can never lose anything that is good, never lose love or the memories of great happiness because they are true. I've come to the conclusion that only the eternal is real! And that means qualities that one loves in people – their humour, generosity, honour, kindness, gentleness etc. are the reality: and can never die. They are the identity of the one one loves.

JOYCE GRENFELL

from JOURNAL OF A SOUL

Death is the future for everyone. It is the Last Post of this life and the Reveille of the next.

Death is the end of our present life, it is the parting from loved ones, it is setting out into the unknown. We overcome death by accepting it as the will of a loving God, by finding Him in it.

Death, like birth, is only a transformation, another birth. When we may die we shall change our state, that is all. In faith in God, it is as easy and natural as going to sleep here and waking up there.

POPE JOHN XXIII

from WINNIE-THE-POOH

IN WHICH PIGLET MEETS A HEFFALUMP

One day, when Christopher Robin and Winnie-the-Pooh and Piglet were all talking together, Christopher Robin finished the mouthful he was eating and said carelessly: 'I saw a Heffalump to-day, Piglet.'

'What was it doing?' asked Piglet.

'Just lumping along,' said Christopher Robin. 'I don't think it saw *me*.'

'I saw one once,' said Piglet. 'At least, I think I did,' he said. 'Only perhaps it wasn't.'

'So did I,' said Pooh, wondering what a Heffalump was like.

'You don't often see them,' said Christopher Robin carelessly.

'Not now,' said Piglet.

'Not at this time of year,' said Pooh.

Then they all talked about something else, until it was time for Pooh and Piglet to go home together. At first as they stumped along the path which edged the Hundred Acre Wood, they didn't say much to each other; but when they came to the stream, and had helped each other across the stepping stones, and were able to walk side by side again over the heather, they began to talk in a friendly way about this and that, and Piglet said, 'If you see what I mean, Pooh,' and Pooh said, 'It's just what I think myself, Piglet,' and Piglet said, 'But, on the other hand, Pooh, we must remember,' and Pooh said, 'Quite true, Piglet, although I had forgotten it for the moment.' And then, just as they came to the Six Pine Trees, Pooh looked round to see that nobody else was listening, and said in a very solemn voice:

'Piglet, I have decided something.'

'What have you decided, Pooh?'

'I have decided to catch a Heffalump.'

Pooh nodded his head several times as he said this, and waited for Piglet to say 'How?' or 'Pooh, you couldn't!' or something helpful of that sort, but Piglet said nothing. The fact was Piglet was wishing that *he* had thought about it first.

'I shall do it,' said Pooh, after waiting a little longer, 'by means of a trap. And it must be a Cunning Trap, so you will have to help me, Piglet.'

'Pooh,' said Piglet, feeling quite happy again now, 'I will.' And then he said, 'How shall we do it?' and Pooh said, 'That's just it. How?' And then they sat down together to think it out.

A.A. MILNE

LETTER TO HIS DYING FATHER, 4 April 1787

As death is the true goal of our existence, I have found such close relations with this best and truest friend of mankind that this image is not only no longer frightening, but is indeed soothing and consoling; and I thank My Lord that he has granted me the opportunity of knowing that this is the key which unlocks the door to our true state of happiness.

At night I never lie down in my bed without thinking that perhaps I shall not live to see the next day; and yet not one of my acquaintances could say that in my intercourse with him I am stubborn or morose, and for this source of happiness I thank my Creator every day, and wish with all my heart the same for my fellow creatures.

WOLFGANG AMADEUS MOZART

from THE LAST DAYS OF SOCRATES

(Socrates has been condemned to death, and Plato reports him speaking to the jury.)

I suspect that this thing that has happened to me is a blessing, and we are quite mistaken in supposing death to be an evil . . . Death is one of two things. Either it is annihilation, and the dead have no consciousness of anything; or, as we are told, it is really a change: a migration of the soul from this place to another. Now if there is no consciousness but only a dreamless sleep, death must be a marvellous gain. I suppose that if anyone were told to pick out the night on which he slept so soundly as not even to dream, and then to compare it with all the other nights and days of his life, and then were told to say, after due consideration how many better and happier days and nights than this he had spent in the course of his life – well, I think that the Great King himself, to say nothing of any private person, would find these days and nights easy to count in comparison with the rest. If death is like this, then, I call it gain; because the whole of time, if you look at it in this way, can be regarded as no more than one single night. If, on the other hand, death is a removal from here to some other place, and if what we are told is true, that all the dead are there, what greater blessing could there be than this, gentlemen? If on arrival in the other world, beyond the reach of our so-called justice, one will find that the true judges who are said to preside in those courts, Minos and Rhadamanthys and Aecus and Triptolemus and all those other half-divinities who were upright in their earthly life, would that be an unrewarding journey? Put it in this way: how much would one of you give to meet Orpheus and Musaeus, Hesiod and Homer? I am willing to die ten times over if this account is true. It would be a specially interesting experience for me to join them there, to meet Palamedes and Ajax the son of Telamon and any other heroes of the old days who met their death through an unfair trial, and to compare my fortunes with theirs – it would be rather amusing, I think –; and above all I should like to spend my time there, as here, in examining and searching people's minds, to find out who is really wise among them, and who only thinks that he is. What would one not give, gentlemen, to be able to question the leader of that great host against Troy, or Odysseus, or Sisyphus, or the thousands of other men and women whom one could mention. To talk and mix and argue with whom would be unimaginable happiness? At any rate I presume that they do not put one to death there for such conducts; because apart from the other happiness in which their world surpasses ours, they are now immortal for the rest of time, if what we are told is true . . .

Now it is time that we were going, I to die and you to live; but which of us has the happier prospect is unknown to anyone but God.

PLATO

from ST GEORGE'S DAY ADDRESS, 22 April 1964

For the unbroken life of the English nation over a thousand years and more is a phenomenon unique in history, the product of a specific set of circumstances like those which in biology are supposed to start by chance a new line of evolution. Institutions which elsewhere are recent and artificial creations, appear in England almost as works of nature, spontaneous and unquestioned. The deepest instinct of the Englishman – how the word 'instinct' keeps forcing itself in again and again! – is for continuity; he never acts more freely nor innovates more boldly than when he most is conscious of conserving or even of reacting.

From this continuous life of a united people in its island home spring, as from the soil of England, all that is peculiar in the gifts and the achievements of the English nation, its laws, its literature, its freedom, its self-discipline. All its impact on the outer world, in earlier colonies, in later *pax Britannica*, in government and lawgiving, in commerce and in thought, has flowed from impulses generated here. And this continuous and continuing life of England is symbolized and expressed, as by nothing else, by the English kingship. English it is, for all the leeks and thistles and shamrocks, the Stuarts and the Hanoverians, for all the titles grafted upon it here and elsewhere, 'her other realms and territories', Headships of Commonwealths, and what not. The stock that received all these grafts is English, the sap that rises through it to the extremities rises from roots in English earth, the earth of England's history.

We in our day ought well to guard, as highly to honour, the parent stem of England, and its royal talisman; for we know not what branches yet that wonderful tree will have the power to put forth. The danger is not always violence and force: them we have withstood before and can again. The peril can also be indifference and humbug, which might squander the accumulated wealth of tradition and devalue our sacred symbolism to achieve some cheap compromise or some evanescent purpose.

These are not thoughts for every day, nor words for every company; but on St George's eve, in the Society of St George, may we not fitly think and speak them, to renew and strengthen in ourselves the resolves and the loyalties which English reserve keeps otherwise and best in silence?

ENOCH POWELL

L'art est ce qu'il y a de plus réel, la plus austère école de la vie, et le vrai Jugement dernier.

MARCEL PROUST

[83]

from À LA RECHERCHE DU TEMPS PERDU

The truths which the intellect apprehends directly in the world of full and unimpeded light have something less profound, less necessary than those which life communicates to us against our will in an impression which is material because it enters us through the senses, but yet has a spiritual meaning which it is possible for us to extract.

As for the inner book of unknown symbols, if I tried to read them no one could help me with any rules, for to read them is an act of creation in which no one can do our work for us or even collaborate with us. For instinct dictates our duty and the intellect supplies us with pretexts for evading it. But excuses have no place in art and intentions count for nothing: at every moment the artist has to listen to his instinct, and it is this that makes art the most real of all things, the most austere school of life, the true last judgement.

MARCEL PROUST

A READING

Let us be contented with what has happened to us and thankful for all we have been spared. Let us accept the natural order in which we move. Let us reconcile ourselves to the mysterious rhythm of our destinies, such as they must be in this world of space and time. Let us treasure our joys but not bewail our sorrows. The glory of light cannot exist without its shadow. Life is a whole and good and ill must be accepted together. The journey has been enjoyable and well worth making.

ANON.

INSPIRATION

from RED CLOUD SPEAKS

Gaze upon the face of a flower and note its beauty. Inhale the perfume which rises gently to your nostrils. In that moment of silent admiration you reach God's garden and your spiritual home. For home with God can only be in beauty, whatever way you seek it.

Perhaps you will find it on a summer's evening as you gaze across the sky, the sun setting in its beauteous colourings and the gentle moon rising. Your heart and soul with wonderment filled with the beauty of God's kingdom and its blessing. Thus you find inspiration, for you are awakening and sensing God.

WENDY SOMES

from THE CHRISTIAN CENTURIES

'THE SIBYL OF THE RHINE'

A little more than forty years after Urban the eloquent had died in Rome . . . a highly-gifted middle-aged German woman who was small in stature, did not like cats, was unafraid of popes or of emperors, and is acclaimed by some as the unsung prophetess of the twentieth century, had a vision.

> *In the year of Our Lord 1141, when I was forty-two and seven months, I saw a mass of fiery light of the greatest brightness pouring down from the heavens. It enveloped my brain and my heart was kindled with a flame that did not burn me but warmed me as the sun warms the earth.*
>
> *From that moment on I knew and understood the meaning of the Psalms and the Gospels – as well as the other books of the Old and New Testaments. By 'understood' I do not mean that I was suddenly expert in evaluating the text, dividing the syllables and working out the cases and tenses. No, I understood the meaning.*

The visionary was Hildegard of Bingen – musician, ecologist, dramatist, apothecary, herbalist, cosmologist, preacher and prophetess. The fireball vision was by no means her first vision but it was a turning point in her life. It dispelled her doubts and gave her the courage to write and teach with a verve and a conviction which would make many uncomfortable.

Hildegard has always been controversial. In her own time, she was accused of hysteria and fraud. She organized the first-ever monastic strike. Nowadays she is hailed by some as the first female voice questioning the patriarchy of the Church. Others point to her statement that all science is of God as either an example of medieval naivety or as an insight which the scientific world is slowly coming to terms with . . .

Hildegard's convents enabled her to reach conclusions which Dame Felicitas Corrigan believes many of us are only slowly coming to today. Hildegard says the earth is mother of all that is natural, mother of all that is human. Men and women are sprung from the earth which gave substance to the incarnation of the Son of God. She sees this all against a background of revelation which she had learned in her monastery and nowhere else. She talks of the sweating power of the earth, of the need to stay juicy green. Green is one of her favourite words. Be moist, be joyful, she says. She tells people to become a flowering orchard. And she proclaims the beauty of sexuality and marriage. She says that the ultimate sin that man is committing is a sin against God's creation. If we injure the earth, we shall destroy all life including our own. If we ill-treat and violate the elements of the cosmos, misuse the privilege that is ours, then, she says, God's justice will permit creation to punish humanity. Dame Felicitas believes this is what we are seeing now, with the rivers polluted and the air polluted and acid rain and the nuclear threat. Hildegard is remarkable as being the prophet of the twentieth century, the prophet of the ecological age. She saw all creation, the whole cosmos, and this is something we have to recover. She saw that we had to return to a spiritual outlook of gratitude to God for this wonderful cosmos in which we live and she foresaw an age of renewal of the earth as a bio-spiritual planet. She said, if we do not repent, then God's justice, nature itself, will permit creation to punish humanity. She has the sense of earth as a region of delight – a dream for today's world as well as Hildegard's.

FRANCES GUMLEY AND BRIAN REDHEAD

from THE INSPIRATION OF LANDSCAPE: ARTISTS IN NATIONAL PARKS

NORTHUMBERLAND

'What made me choose Northumberland of the ten National Parks was my sight of it in other summers,' says Peter Greenham. 'The clouds seemed to be as solid and sharp as the trees, and the trees as exalted and forbidding as the sky.'

G. M. Trevelyan, the historian, whose family occupied Wallington Hall, the finest house in the Wansbeck Valley, was of the same opinion. 'The clouds in Northumberland,' he once wrote, 'are like an army waiting on the horizon.'

'Northumberland is a dark country, except in winter, when the sun shines through the bare trees. It is one of the few places in England where one no longer seems to be trapped in a small island.'

He was right. Northumberland is like a kingdom in itself, with its own geography, its own history, and its own freedom. The Romans drew the line at it, putting a wall between their conquests and everything to the north. But between that wall and the River Tweed a whole civilization flourished . . .

It feels as it must always have felt with the clouds on the horizon and the wide sky. It is too large a landscape to be diminished by the activities upon it. Equally, those who have acted out their lives here have an heroic dimension. The great Christians, Paulinus, Aidan, Cuthbert, Bede. The great warriors, like James, Earl of Douglas and Harry Hotspur. There have been villainies too and acts of despair. But it is as if everyone counted, and the landscape counted most of all.

It is the continuing inspiration of everything that has gone on here. A landscape that cannot be ignored, amended or deceived.

If Hadrian were to return, or Harry Hotspur or Charles Trevelyan, they would not feel out of place. Northumberland is one of the few places in the world where what went before seems like part of your own life and not something distant, remote or bewildering. The space makes time relative. It is not a question of the old and the new, but of episodes of the same. It would come as no surprise on Whin Sill if a Roman soldier were to say, 'good evening'. He always did.

This continuity is the character of the place, the confirmation that people have gone about their business here over the centuries under the same forbidding sky.

BRIAN REDHEAD (*editor*)

✳

[87]

from À LA RECHERCHE DU TEMPS PERDU

People do not die for us immediately, but remain bathed in a sort of aura of life which bears no relation to true immortality but through which they continue to occupy our thoughts in the same way as when they were alive. It is as though they were travelling abroad.

MARCEL PROUST

EPITAPH FOR VICTOR

from THE DAILY EXPRESS

He towered 18ft above our troubles. He rose above Northern Ireland, Rhodesia, a bread strike, and the deaths of Marc Bolan and Maria Callas. He blocked telephone lines, jammed the postal system, and called out the Navy. The very earth shook when he fell. For six anxious days, our thoughts, our news bulletins, and our prayers have been weighed down by a one ton 15-year-old giraffe. Advice, and tears, have poured into his sick-pen from a nation united, all eyes on the skyline, in their grief. Winch him, float him, excavate him, do any damned thing, at any cost, but get him to his feet, cried strong men in their anguish. 'But why can't he just get UP, mum,' literally wept children, in their innocence. And every night, and morning, the bulletins were put out on TV and in newspapers. He's rallying. He's sinking. He has a 50–50 chance. We hunched round the reports, breathlessly waiting, like those British who remember the world-famous bulletin on George V: 'The King's life is drawing peacefully to its close'.

Before The Fall, he was just another giraffe. One of those wobbly-legged fur jigsaw puzzles you chuckle at at the zoo. After The Fall, he became a nation's hero. He died for love of a woman. Or rather, great-hearted creature and Father of 18 calves that he was, he died for love of three women. He was Romeo to their Juliets. Antony to their Cleopatras. And his final, tragic moments, as his mighty frame lay stricken, and his own dumb tears rolled from under his yard-brush eyelashes, filled us with pity and terror for him. Because the whole country, God bless us, rose to him. And to the grandeur of his fight for life. Who but the British could down tears, and all but tools, for a giraffe? Who but this nation of shopkeepers, cat-lovers and dog-walkers, could forget their own social and economic fears, hoping for a miracle for Victor? In Russia, he would have been shot the moment he slipped, as unproductive. In America, they would have banned the too meaningful showing of his violent animal love, and possible traumatic death, on TV. In the rest of Europe, they'd have shrugged and sent for the dust cart. Only the British could close ranks, shoulder to shoulder, and cheek-to-wet-cheek, to battle with an almost World War Two sense of comradeship, for the life of a giraffe. Now Victor has gone, and the horizon is suddenly shockingly blank. And it's time to turn back to living, and violence, and inflation. Today, the complete strangers who met and talked in the street last night, to tell one another – 'he's dead, did you hear on the news he's dead' will stop talking together. Re-start self-involved living. Try to forget it – like Christmas, once it's over.

But the fallen Victor has not died in vain. He restored at least a little faith in British nature.

JEAN ROOK

from MEMOIRS OF CHILDHOOD AND YOUTH

I always think that we all live, spiritually, by what others have given us in the significant hours of our life. These significant hours do not announce themselves as coming, but arrive unexpected. Nor do they make a great show of themselves; they pass almost unperceived. Often, indeed, their significance comes home to us first as we look back, just as the beauty of a piece of music or of a landscape often strikes us first in our recollection of it. Much that has become our own in gentleness, modesty, kindness, willingness to forgive, in veracity, loyalty, resignation under suffering, we owe to people in whom we have seen or experienced these virtues at work, sometimes in a great matter, sometimes in a small. A thought which had become act sprang into us like a spark, and lighted a new flame within us.

If we had before us those who have thus been a blessing to us, and could tell them how it came about, they would be amazed to learn what passed over from their life into ours.

ALBERT SCHWEITZER

from WHO'S GOD

Life holds an infinite complexity of patterns –
Of love and truth, beauty and diversity,
Of sorrow and reconciliation, peace and joy –
Patterns of exquisite clarity and symmetry and perfection.
Do not these patterns add up to a Grand Design?
And does not a Grand Design postulate a Designer?
Is this the Ultimate Deity – the Master of the Universe?
Does He encompass all that is incomprehensible to all men –
The totality of the unknown and the unknowable?
And is He the same God as the good in the spirit of man?
I still don't know the answers to all these questions,
But it's of no consequence at all to anyone but me.

PETER SCOTT

from THE TIME MACHINE

The darkness grew apace; a cold wind began to grow in freshening gusts from the east, and the showering white flakes in the air increased in number. From the edge of the sea came a ripple and whisper. Beyond these lifeless sounds the world was silent. Silent? It would be hard to convey the stillness of it. All the sounds of man, the bleatings of sheep, the cries of birds, the hum of insects, the stir that makes the background of our lives – all that was over . . .

A horror of this great darkness came on me . . .

H. G. WELLS

from LOVE LETTERS ON BLUE PAPER

Synopsis:

Victor, a retired Yorkshire trade union leader is dying of leukaemia. He doesn't want to tell his wife, Sonia; instead he calls to his bedside the younger Maurice Stapleton, Professor of Art, his protégé, in whom he confides and with whom he attempts to confront 'the big questions'.

Sonia writes letters to him with neither beginnings nor endings, posts, and delivers them to him in the mornings with his other post. Neither of them talk about the letters.

The letters begin as simple recollections and end as passionate declarations. Through them she reveals a love she was unable to express and, through recalling their life together, prepares him for death.

Sonia:

There will be my darling one, I know it, a blinding light a painful light when suddenly the lie will fall away from truth. Everything will make its own and lovely sense, trust me trust me. It won't be logical or happy, this sense, but clear. Everything will become clear. Trust me. Contradictions won't cease to be contradictions, I don't say that, but nor will they any longer confuse. I'm not promising all will seem to have been good, but evil won't bewilder you as it once did. Trust me, I adore you. And with this blinding light will come an ending to all pain. The body's pain the heart's pain the pain in your soul. All in a second. Less than a second. Less than less than a second. I'm sure of it. That's how it will be for us all, I've always known it. No matter how it happens to us. Accident, torture . . . Suddenly at the top of our energies, quietly in bed. There will come this flash, this light of a colour we've never seen before. It's a glorious moment beloved. Even for the simpleton, even for him, his foolishness falls away just as from the madman his madness falls away. In the instant they know death so they know truth. In the blinding light of truth they know death. One and the same. I promise you, trust me, love O my love O my Victor O my heart.

ARNOLD WESKER

from THE WIMBLEDON POISONER

Henry Farr did not, precisely, decide to murder his wife. It was simply that he could think of no other way of prolonging her absence from him indefinitely.

He had quite often, in the past, when she was being more than usually irritating, had fantasies about her death. She hurtled over cliffs in flaming cars or was brutally murdered on her way to the dry cleaners. But Henry was never actually responsible for the event. He was at the graveside looking mournful and interesting. Or he was coping with his daughter as she roamed the now deserted house, trying not to look as if he was glad to have the extra space. But he was never actually the instigator.

Once he had got the idea of killing her (and at first this fantasy did not seem very different from the reveries in which he wept by her open grave, comforted by young, fashionably dressed women) it took some time to appreciate that this scenario was of quite a different type from the others. It was a dream that could, if he so wished, become reality.

One Friday afternoon in September, he thought about strangling her. The Wimbledon Strangler. He liked that idea. He could see Edgar Lustgarten narrowing his eyes threateningly at the camera, as he paced out the length of Maple Drive. 'But Henry Farr,' Lustgarten was saying, 'with the folly of the criminal, the supreme arrogance of the murderer, had forgotten one vital thing. The shred of fibre that was to send Henry Farr to the gallows was –'

What was he thinking of? They didn't hang people any more. They wrote long, bestselling paperback books about them. Convicted murderers, especially brutal and disgusting ones, were followed around by as many *paparazzi* as the royal family. Their thoughts on life and love and literature were published in Sunday newspapers. Television documentary-makers asked them, respectfully, about exactly how they felt when they hacked their aged mothers to death or disembowelled a neighbour's child. This was the age of the murderer. And wasn't Edgar Lustgarten dead?

He wouldn't, anyway, be known as the Wimbledon Strangler, but as Henry Farr, cold-blooded psychopath. Or, better still, just Farr, cold-blooded psychopath. Henry liked the idea of being a cold-blooded psychopath. He pictured himself in a cell, as the television cameras rolled. He wouldn't moan and stutter and twitch the way most of these murderers did. He would give a clear, coherent account of how and why he had stabbed, shot, strangled, gassed or electrocuted her. 'Basically,' he would say to the camera, his gestures as urgent and incisive as those of any other citizen laying down the law on television, 'basically I'm a very passionate man. I love and I hate. And when love turns to hate, for me, you know, that's it. I simply had no wish for her to live. I stand by that decision.' Here he would suddenly stare straight into the camera lens in the way he had seen so many politicians do, and say, 'I challenge any red-blooded Englishman who really feels. Who has passion. Not to do the same. When love dies, it dies.'

Hang on. Was he a red-blooded Englishman or a cold-blooded psychopath? Or was he a bit of both? Was it possible to combine the two roles?

Either way, however he did it (and he was becoming increasingly sure that it was a good idea), his life was going to be a lot more fun.

NIGEL WILLIAMS

from DEVOTING

No man is an island, entire of itself; every man is a piece of the continent, a part of the main. The death of one diminishes all. For all are bound together in the bundle of life. We are involved in Mankind. Yet while there is time, we look with thankfulness upon the broad acres of good earth, the handiwork of the Creator who makes us fellow-workers with himself, and upon the works of men in the industries of this and every land, and we pray: Almighty God, Maker of all things, who has placed thy creatures necessary for the use of man in diverse lands: Grant that all men and nations needing one another may be knit together in one bond of mutual service, to share their diverse riches. Prosper thou the work of our hands upon us, O prosper thou our handiwork, O Lord, our Heavenly Father.

JOHN DONNE

from CELEBRATING FRIENDSHIP

What a lovely party! And how much she must have enjoyed it! When's the next Memorial Service?

SYBIL THORNDIKE

Prayers

Our Father, who art in heaven, hallowed by the Name. Thy kingdom come, thy will be done, on earth as it is in heaven. Give us this day our daily bread. And forgive us our trespasses, as we forgive those who trespass against us. And lead us not into temptation, but deliver us from evil: For thine is the kingdom, the power, and the glory, for ever and ever. Amen.

∽

Almighty God, Father of all mercies and giver of all comfort: deal graciously, we pray thee, with those who mourn, that casting every care on thee, they may know the consolation of thy love; through Jesus Christ our Lord. Amen.

∽

O Father of all, we pray to thee for those whom we love, but see no longer. Grant them thy peace; let light perpetual shine upon them; and in thy loving wisdom and almighty power work in them the good purpose of thy perfect will; through Jesus Christ our Lord. Amen.

∽

O Heavenly Father, who in thy Son, Jesus Christ, hast given us a true faith, and a sure hope: Help us, we pray thee, to live as those who believe and trust in the Communion of Saints, the Forgiveness of Sins, and the Resurrection to Life everlasting; and strengthen this faith and hope in us all the days of our life; through the love of thy Son, Jesus Christ our Saviour. Amen.

∽

O God, who holdest all souls in life and callest them unto thee as seemeth best: we give them back, dear God, to thee who gavest them to us. But as thou didst not lose them in the giving, so we do not lose them by their return. For not as the world giveth, givest thou, O Lord of souls: that which thou givest thou takest away: for life is eternal, and love is immortal, and death is only the horizon, and the horizon is nothing save the limit of our sight.

Lift us up, O God, that we may see further; cleanse our eyes that we may see more clearly; draw us closer to thee that we may know ourselves nearer to our beloved who are with thee. And, as thou dost prepare a place for us, prepare us for that happy place, that where thou art and they are, we too may be, in thine eternal and unending glory. Amen.

∽

Soul of Christ, sanctify me,
Body of Christ, save me,
Blood of Christ, refresh me,
Water from the side of Christ, wash me,
Passion of Christ, strengthen me,
O good Jesus, hear me,
Within your wounds hide me.
Let me never be separated from you,
From the powers of darkness defend me,
In the hour of my death call me,
And bid me come to you,
That with your saints I may praise you
For ever and ever. Amen.

ANIMA CHRISTI

∽

Holy Spirit, Spirit of the Living God,
you breathe in us
on all that is inadequate and fragile.

You make living water spring even
from our hurts themselves. And
through you, the valley of tears
becomes a place of wellsprings.

So, in an inner life
with neither beginning nor end,
your continual presence
makes new freshness break through. Amen.

BROTHER ROGER OF TAIZÉ

∽

God grant us the serenity
to accept the things we cannot change,
the courage to change the things we can,
and the wisdom to know the difference. Amen.

REINHOLD NIEBUHR

Almighty God,
when evil has done its worst and wickedness has spent
its force in death –
you come to us – the Father of a crucified Son:
in Him you have given us the key to your kingdom.
Let not anger cloud our judgement,
nor frustration corrode our faith;
Let resolve for peace and respect for truth
be the ground on which we fight, and
care and kindness the weapons we wield:
that evil may not drag us down,
but your Spirit raise us up;
for, in spite of all, the kingdom, the power
and the glory are yours now and forever. Amen.

REVEREND STEPHEN OLIVER

Thanks be unto thee, O Christ,
   because thou hast broken for us
     the bonds of sin
   and brought us into fellowship
     with the Father.
Thanks be unto thee, O Christ,
   because thou hast overcome death
     and opened to us
     the gates of eternal life.
Thanks be unto thee, O Christ,
   because where two or three are gathered together
     in thy Name
   there art thou in the midst of them.
Thanks be unto thee, O Christ,
   because thou ever livest
   to make intercession for us.

For these and all other benefits
of thy mighty resurrection,
thanks be unto thee, O Christ. Amen.

∽

Preserve us, O Lord, while waking, and guard us while sleeping, that awake we may watch with Christ, and asleep we may rest in peace. Amen.

ANTIPHON, ORDER FOR COMPLINE

∽

Lord, have mercy upon us.
Christ, have mercy upon us.
Lord, have mercy upon us.

∽

Bring us, O Lord God, at our last awakening into the house and gate of heaven; to enter into that gate and dwell in that house, where there shall be no darkness nor dazzling, but one equal light; no noise nor silence, but one equal music; no fears nor hopes, but one equal possession; no ends, nor beginnings, but one equal eternity; in the habitations of thy glory and dominion, world without end. Amen.

JOHN DONNE

∽

O Lord, support us all the day long of this troublous life, until the shades lengthen, and the evening comes, the busy world is hushed, the fever of life is over, and our work is done. Then, Lord, in thy mercy, grant us safe lodging, a holy rest, and peace at the last: through Jesus Christ our Lord. Amen.

JOHN HENRY NEWMAN

∽

O Eternal Lord God, who holdest all souls in life: We beseech thee to shed forth upon thy whole Church in Paradise and on earth the bright beams of thy light and heavenly comfort: and grant that we, following the good example of those who have loved and served thee here and are now at rest, may at the last enter with them into the fulness of thine unending joy; through Jesus Christ our Lord. Amen.

~

Almighty God, Father of all mercies, we thine unworthy servants do give thee most humble and hearty thanks for all thy goodness and loving kindness to us and to all men. We bless thee for our creation, preservation, and all the blessings of this life. But, above all, for thine inestimable love in the redemption of the world by our Lord Jesus Christ; for the means of grace, and for the hope of glory. And, we beseech thee, give us that due sense of all thy mercies, that our hearts may be unfeignedly thankful, and that we shew forth thy praise, not only with our lips but in our lives: by giving up ourselves to thy service, and by walking before thee in holiness and righteousness all our days; through Jesus Christ our Lord, to whom with thee and the Holy Ghost be all honour and glory, world without end. Amen.

~

O God, who by thy Son, Jesus Christ, hast set up on earth a Kingdom of holiness to measure its strength against all others; make faith to prevail over fear, and righteousness over force, truth over the lie, and love and concord over all things; through Jesus Christ, our Lord. Amen.

~

We bring before thee, O Lord, the griefs and perils of peoples and nations; the necessities of the homeless, the helplessness of the aged and weak; the pains of the sick and injured; the sorrows of the bereaved; comfort and relieve them, O merciful Father, according to their several needs; for the sake of thy Son, our Saviour Jesus Christ. Amen.

~

Lord, make us instruments of thy peace.
    Where there is hatred, let us sow love;
    Where there is injury, pardon;
    Where there is discord, union;
    Where there is doubt, faith;

Where there is despair, hope;
Where there is darkness, light;
Where there is sadness, joy;
For thy mercy and for thy truth's sake. Amen.

ST FRANCIS OF ASSISI

∽

O God, the physician of men and nations, the restorer of the years that have been destroyed, look upon the distractions of the world, and be pleased to complete the work of thy healing hand. Draw all men unto thee, and one to another by the hands of thy love; make thy Church one, and fill it with thy Spirit, that by thy power it may unite the world in a sacred brotherhood of nations wherein justice and mercy, truth and freedom, may flourish, and thou mayest ever be glorified, through Jesus Christ our Lord. Amen.

∽

Eternal Father, source of life and light, whose love extends to all people, all creatures, all things: grant us that reverence for life which becomes those who believe in you, lest we despise it, degrade it, or come callously to destroy it. Rather let us save it, secure it, and sanctify it, after the example of your Son, Jesus Christ our Lord. Amen.

∽

O Lord God, when thou givest to thy servants to endeavour any great matter, grant us also to know that it is not the beginning but the continuing of the same until it be thoroughly finished which yieldeth the true glory; through him that for the finishing of thy work laid down his life, our redeemer, Jesus Christ. Amen.

SIR FRANCIS DRAKE

∽

O Holy Spirit, whose presence is liberty, grant us that freedom of the spirit, which will not fear to tread in unknown ways, nor be held back by misgivings of ourselves and fear of others. Ever beckon us forward to the place of thy will which is also the place of thy power, O ever-leading, ever-loving Lord. Amen.

∽

Eternal God and Father, accept our thanks and praise for all that you have done for us. We thank you for the splendour of the whole creation, for the beauty of this world, for the wonder of life, and for the mystery of love. We thank you for the blessing of family and friends, and for the loving care which surrounds us on every side. We thank you for setting us tasks which demand our best efforts, and for leading us to accomplishments which satisfy and delight us. Above all, we thank you for your Son, Jesus Christ; for the truth of his Word and the example of his life; for his dying, through which he overcame death; and for his rising to life again, through which we are raised to new life in your kingdom. Grant us the gift of your Spirit, that we may know him and make him known; and may so live from day to day in the knowledge of your love and goodness, that at all times and in all places, we may give thanks to you through the same Jesus Christ our Lord. Amen.

May the love of the Lord Jesus draw us to himself; May the power of the Lord Jesus strengthen us in his service; May the joy of the Lord Jesus fill our souls; and may the blessing of God Almighty, the Father, the Son, and the Holy Spirit, be with you and abide with you always. Amen.

WILLIAM TEMPLE

Go forward in thy journey from this world, O Christian soul,
In the name of God the Father Almighty who created thee,
In the name of Jesus Christ who suffered for thee,
In the name of the Holy Ghost who strengthens thee,
In communion with the blessed Saints, and aided by Angels
and Archangels, and all the armies of the heavenly host.
May thy portion this day be peace, and thy dwelling in the
heavenly Jerusalem. Amen.

Go forth into the world in peace; be of good courage; hold fast to that which is good; render to no man evil for evil; strengthen the faint hearted; support the weak; help the afflicted; honour all men, love and serve the Lord, rejoicing in the power of the Holy Spirit; and the blessing of God Almighty, Father, Son, and Holy Ghost, be with you, in your homes and with your loved ones, this day and for evermore. Amen.

O Lord, you have given us your word for a light to shine upon our path; grant us so to meditate on that word, and to follow its teaching, that we may find in it the light that shines more and more until the perfect day; through Jesus Christ our Lord. Amen.

۩

We thank thee, O God, for a life lived in human charity with thine earthly world. Rejoice his soul with thy presence and remember not his sins which at any time he committed. For although he hath sinned, he ever had a zeal for thee, the creator of all things. Let the heavens be open to him. Let thine angels rejoice with him. Receive thy servant into thy Kingdom from which all sorrow and sadness is banished: and with the souls of the faithful may he be made partaker of thine everlasting glory. Amen.

۩

If I should die and leave you here awhile,
Be not like others, sore undone, who keep
Long vigils by silent dust, and weep.
For my sake, turn again to life and smile,
Nerving thy heart and trembling hand to do
Something to comfort weaker hearts than thine.
Complete these dear unfinished tasks of mine
And I perchance may therein comfort you!

A. PRICE HUGHES

۩

I would be true for there are those who trust me,
I would be pure for there are those who care,
I would be strong for there is much to suffer,
I would be brave for there is much to dare,
I would be friend of all, the foe, the friendless
I would be giving and forget the gift
I would be humble for I know my weakness
I would look up, and laugh, and love, and live.

ANON.

۩

See that ye hold fast the heritage we leave you, yea and teach your children its value, that never in the coming centuries their hearts may fail them, or their hands grow weak . . .

SIR FRANCIS DRAKE

Let everyone cry out to God and lift our heart up to God, as if we were hanging by a hair, and a tempest were raging to the very heart of heaven, and we were at a loss for what to do, and there were hardly time to cry out. It is a time when no counsel, indeed, can help anyone and we have no refuge save to remain in our loneliness and lift our eyes and our heart up and cry out to God. And this should be done at all times, for in the world a person is in great danger.

CHASIDIC

Everything is given on pledge and a net is cast for all living. The shop is open, the shopkeeper gives credit, the account is open and the hand writes and whoever wishes to borrow may come and borrow, but the collectors go round every day and exact payment from us with our consent or without it, and their claims are justified and the judgement is a judgement of truth. Yet everything is prepared for the feast!

PIRQE AVOT

God of our strength, in our weakness help us; in our sorrow comfort us; in our confusion guide us. Without You our lives are nothing; with You there is fullness of life for evermore.

O Lord, the first and the last, the beginning and the end: you who were with us at our birth, be with us through our life; you who are with us through our life, be with us at our death; and, because your mercy will not leave us then, grant that we die not, but rise to the life everlasting.

PAULINE WEBB

Strengthen now the bands of love which unite us all in thee and in death divide us not; for the sake of Jesus Christ our Lord. Amen.

☙

Teach us, Good Lord, to serve thee as Thou deservest,
To give, and not to count the cost;
To fight, and not to heed the wounds,
To toil, and not to seek for rest;
To labour, and not to ask for any reward,
Save that of knowing that we do Thy will.

ST IGNATIUS LOYOLA

☙

The grace of our Lord Jesus Christ, and the love of God, and the fellowship of the Holy Spirit, be with us all evermore. Amen.

☙

Deep peace of the running wave to you.
Deep peace of the flowing air to you.
Deep peace of the quiet earth to you.
Deep peace of the shining stars to you.

CELTIC BENEDICTION

☙

The peace of God, which passeth all understanding, keep your hearts and minds in the knowledge and love of God, and of his Son Jesus Christ our Lord: and the blessing of God Almighty, the Father, the Son, and the Holy Ghost, be amongst you and remain with you always. Amen.

☙

May God give to you and to all those you love his comfort and his peace, his light and his joy, in this world and the next; and the blessing of God almighty, the Father, the Son and the Holy Spirit rest upon you and remain with you always. Amen.

☙

Hymns

And did those feet in ancient time
  Walk upon England's mountains green?
And was the holy Lamb of God
  On England's pleasant pastures seen?

And did the countenance divine
  Shine forth upon our clouded hills?
And was Jerusalem builded here
  Among those dark satanic mills?

Bring me my bow of burning gold!
  Bring me my arrows of desire!
Bring me my spear! O clouds, unfold!
  Bring me my chariot of fire!

I will not cease from mental fight,
  Nor shall my sword sleep in my hand,
Till we have built Jerusalem
  In England's green and pleasant land.

WILLIAM BLAKE
Hubert Parry: 'Jerusalem'

Immortal, invisible, God only wise,
In light inaccessible hid from our eyes,
Most blessèd, most glorious, the Ancient of Days,
Almighty, victorious, thy great name we praise.

Unresting, unhasting, and silent as light,
Nor wanting, nor wasting, thou rulest in might;
Thy justice like mountains high-soaring above
Thy clouds which are fountains of goodness and love.

To all life thou givest, to both great and small;
In all life thou livest, the true life of all;
We blossom and flourish as leaves on the tree,
And wither and perish; but naught changeth thee.

Great Father of glory, pure Father of light,
Thine angels adore thee, all veiling their sight;
All laud we would render; O help us to see
'Tis only the splendour of light hideth thee.

WALTER CHALMERS SMITH
'St Denio': Welsh Hymn Melody

Praise, my soul, the King of Heaven,
   To his feet thy tribute bring;
Ransomed, healed, restored, forgiven,
   Who like me his praise should sing?
     Alleluia, alleluia,
Praise the everlasting King.

Praise him for his grace and favour
   To our fathers in distress;
Praise him still the same for ever,
   Slow to chide, and swift to bless:
     Alleluia, alleluia,
   Glorious in his faithfulness.

Father-like, he tends and spares us,
   Well our feeble frame he knows;
In his hands he gently bears us,
   Rescues us from all our foes:
     Alleluia, alleluia,
   Widely as his mercy flows.

Angels, help us to adore him;
   Ye behold him face to face;
Sun and moon, bow down before him,
   Dwellers all in time and space:
     Alleluia, alleluia,
   Praise with us the God of grace.

HENRY FRANCIS LYTE
Psalm 103
John Goss: 'Praise my Soul'

Abide with me; fast falls the eventide;
The darkness deepens; Lord, with me abide!
When other helpers fail, and comforts flee,
Help of the helpless, O abide with me.

Swift to its close ebbs out life's little day;
Earth's joys grow dim, its glories pass away;
Change and decay in all around I see;
O thou who changest not, abide with me.

I need thy presence every passing hour;
What but thy grace can foil the tempter's power?
Who like thyself my guide and stay can be?
Through cloud and sunshine, O abide with me.

I fear no foe with thee at hand to bless;
Ills have no weight, and tears no bitterness.
Where is death's sting? where, grave, thy victory?
I triumph still, if thou abide with me.

Hold thou thy cross before my closing eyes;
Shine through the gloom, and point me to the skies:
Heaven's morning breaks, and earth's vain shadows flee;
In life, in death, O Lord, abide with me!

HENRY FRANCIS LYTE
St Luke 24:29
William Henry Monk: 'Eventide'

Dear Lord and Father of mankind,
    Forgive our foolish ways!
Re-clothe us in our rightful mind,
In purer lives thy service find,
    In deeper reverence praise.

In simple trust like theirs who heard,
    Beside the Syrian sea,
The gracious calling of the Lord,
Let us, like them, without a word
    Rise up and follow thee.

[III]

O Sabbath rest by Galilee!
   O calm of hills above,
Where Jesus knelt to share with thee
The silence of eternity,
   Interpreted by love!

Drop thy still dews of quietness,
   Till all our strivings cease;
Take from our souls the strain and stress,
And let our ordered lives confess
   The beauty of thy peace.

Breathe through the heats of our desire
   Thy coolness and thy balm;
Let sense be dumb, let flesh retire;
Speak through the earthquake, wind, and fire,
   O still small voice of calm!

JOHN GREENLEAF WHITTIER
from 'The Brewing of Soma'
Hubert Parry: 'Repton'

❧

All creatures of our God and King,
Lift up your voice and with us sing
   Alleluia, alleluia!
Thou burning sun with golden beam,
Thou silver moon with softer gleam,
   O praise him, O praise him,
   Alleluia, alleluia, alleluia!

And all ye men of tender heart,
Forgiving others, take your part,
   O sing ye alleluia!
Ye who long pain and sorrow bear,
Praise God and on him cast your care;
   O praise him, O praise him,
   Alleluia, alleluia, alleluia!

And thou, most kind and gentle Death,
Waiting to hush our latest breath,
   O praise him, alleluia!

Thou leadest home the child of God,
And Christ our Lord the way hath trod;
   O praise him, O praise him,
   Alleluia, alleluia, alleluia!

Let all things their Creator bless,
And worship him in humbleness;
   O praise him, alleluia!
Praise, praise the Father, praise the Son,
And praise the Spirit, Three in One;
   O praise him, O praise him,
   Alleluia, alleluia, alleluia!

> WILLIAM HENRY DRAPER
> *St Francis of Assisi: Canticle of the Sun*
> *Ralph Vaughan Williams: 'Lasst Uns Erfreuen'*

He who would valiant be
   'Gainst all disaster,
Let him in constancy
   Follow the Master.
There's no discouragement
Shall make him once relent
His first avowed intent
   To be a pilgrim.

Who so beset him round
   With dismal stories,
Do but themselves confound –
   His strength the more is.
No foes shall stay his might,
Though he with giants fight:
He will make good his right
   To be a pilgrim.

Since, Lord, thou dost defend
   Us with thy Spirit,
We know we at the end
   Shall life inherit.

Then fancies flee away!
I'll fear not what men say,
I'll labour night and day
To be a pilgrim.

JOHN BUNYAN and PERCY DEARMER
Ralph Vaughan Williams: 'Monks Gate'

Come down, O Love divine,
Seek thou this soul of mine,
And visit it with thine own ardour glowing:
O Comforter, draw near,
Within my heart appear,
And kindle it, thy holy flame bestowing.

O let it freely burn,
Till earthly passions turn
To dust and ashes in its heat consuming;
And let thy glorious light
Shine ever on my sight,
And clothe me round, the while my path illuming.

Let holy charity
Mine outward vesture be,
And lowliness become mine inner clothing;
True lowliness of heart,
Which takes the humbler part,
And o'er its own shortcomings weeps with loathing.

And so the yearning strong,
With which the soul will long,
Shall far outpass the power of human telling;
For none can guess its grace,
Till he become the place
Wherein the Holy Spirit makes his dwelling.

BIANCO DA SIENA
tr. R. F. Littledale
Ralph Vaughan Williams: 'Down Ampney'

Guide me, O Thou great Redeemer,
    Pilgrim through this barren land;
I am weak, but Thou art mighty,
    Hold me with Thy powerful hand;
Bread of heaven, bread of heaven,
    Feed me now and evermore.

Open now the crystal fountain,
    Whence the healing streams do flow:
Let the fiery cloudy pillar
    Lead me all my journey through;
Strong Deliverer, strong Deliverer,
    Be thou still my strength and shield.

When I tread the verge of Jordan,
    Bid my anxious fears subside:
Death of death, and hell's destruction,
    Land me safe on Canaan's side;
Songs of praises, songs of praises,
    I will ever give to thee.

WILLIAM WILLIAMS
Sir George Elvey

I vow to thee, my country, all earthly things above,
Entire and whole and perfect, the service of my love:
The love that asks no question, the love that stands the test,
That lays upon the altar the dearest and the best;
The love that never falters, the love that pays the price,
The love that makes undaunted the final sacrifice.

And there's another country, I've heard of long ago,
Most dear to them that love her, most great to them that know;
We may not count her armies, we may not see her King;
Her fortress is a faithful heart, her pride is suffering;
And soul by soul and silently her shining bounds increase,
And her ways are ways of gentleness and all her paths are peace.

CECIL SPRING-RICE
Gustav Holst: 'Thaxted'

Let all the world in every corner sing,
    My God and King.
  The heavens are not too high,
  His praise may thither fly:
  The earth is not too low,
  His praises there may grow.
Let all the world in every corner sing,
    My God and King.

Let all the world in every corner sing,
    My God and King.
  The Church with psalms must shout,
  No door can keep them out;
  But above all, the heart
  Must bear the longest part.
Let all the world in every corner sing,
    My God and King.

GEORGE HERBERT
Basil Harwood: 'Luckington'

Lord of all hopefulness, Lord of all joy,
Whose trust, ever childlike, no cares could destroy,
Be there at our waking, and give us, we pray,
Your bliss in our hearts, Lord, at the break of the day.

Lord of all kindliness, Lord of all grace,
Your hands swift to welcome, your arms to embrace,
Be there at our homing, and give us, we pray,
Your love in our hearts, Lord, at the eve of the day.

Lord of all gentleness, Lord of all calm,
Whose voice is contentment, whose presence is balm,
Be there at our sleeping, and give us, we pray,
Your peace in our hearts, Lord, at the end of the day.

JAN STRUTHER
Cyril V. Taylor: 'Miniver'

The Lord's my Shepherd, I'll not want;
    He makes me down to lie
In pastures green; he leadeth me
    The quiet waters by.

My soul he doth restore again,
    And me to walk doth make
Within the paths of righteousness,
    E'en for his own name's sake.

Yea, though I walk through death's dark vale,
    Yet will I fear none ill;
For thou art with me, and thy rod
    And staff me comfort still.

My table thou hast furnishèd
    In presence of my foes;
My head thou dost with oil anoint,
    And my cup overflows.

Goodness and mercy all my life
    Shall surely follow me;
And in God's house for evermore
    My dwelling-place shall be.

PSALM 23
Jessie Irvine: 'Crimond'

The day thou gavest, Lord, is ended,
The darkness falls at thy behest;
To thee our morning hymns ascended,
Thy praise shall sanctify our rest.

We thank thee that thy Church unsleeping,
While earth rolls onward into light,
Through all the world her watch is keeping,
And rests not now by day or night.

As o'er each continent and island
The dawn leads on another day,
The voice of prayer is never silent,
Nor dies the strain of praise away.

So be it, Lord; thy throne shall never,
Like earth's proud empires, pass away;
Thy Kingdom stands, and grows for ever,
Till all thy creatures own thy sway.

JOHN ELLERTON
Clement Scholefield: 'St Clement'

The King of love my Shepherd is,
Whose goodness faileth never;
I nothing lack if I am his
And he is mine for ever.

Where streams of living water flow
My ransomed soul he leadeth,
And where the verdant pastures grow
With food celestial feedeth.

Perverse and foolish oft I strayed,
But yet in love he sought me,
And on his shoulder gently laid,
And home rejoicing brought me.

In death's dark vale I fear no ill
With thee, dear Lord, beside me;
Thy rod and staff my comfort still,
Thy Cross before to guide me.

Thou spread'st a table in my sight;
Thy unction grace bestoweth;
And O what transport of delight
From thy pure chalice floweth!

And so through all the length of days
Thy goodness faileth never:
Good Shepherd, may I sing thy praise
Within thy house for ever.

HENRY WILLIAMS BAKER
John Bacchus Dykes: 'Dominus Regit Me'

Eternal Father, strong to save,
Whose arm hath bound the restless wave,
Who bidd'st the mighty ocean deep
Its own appointed limits keep:
  O hear us when we cry to thee
  For those in peril on the sea.

O Christ, whose voice the waters heard
And hushed their raging at thy word,
Who walkedst on the foaming deep,
And calm amid the storm didst sleep:
  O hear us when we cry to thee
  For those in peril on the sea.

O Holy Spirit, who didst brood
Upon the waters dark and rude,
And bid their angry tumult cease,
And give, for wild confusion, peace:
  O hear us when we cry to thee
  For those in peril on the sea.

O Trinity of love and power,
Our brethren shield in danger's hour;
From rock and tempest, fire and foe,
Protect them wheresoe'er they go:
  Thus evermore shall rise to thee
  Glad hymns of praise from land and sea.

WILLIAM WHITING
John Bacchus Dykes: 'Melita'

Fight the good fight with all thy might,
Christ is thy Strength and Christ thy Right;
Lay hold on life, and it shall be
Thy joy and crown eternally.

Run the straight race through God's good grace,
Lift up thine eyes, and seek His Face;
Life with its way before us lies,
Christ is the path, and Christ the prize.

Cast care aside, lean on thy Guide;
His boundless mercy will provide;
Trust, and thy trusting soul shall prove
Christ is its life, and Christ its love.

Faint not nor fear, His Arms are near,
He changeth not, and thou art dear;
Only believe, and thou shalt see
That Christ is all in all to thee.

JOHN SAMUEL BEWLEY MONSELL
John Hatton: 'Duke Street'

For all the Saints who from their labours rest,
who thee by faith before the world confest,
thy name, O Jesu, be for ever blest. *Alleluya!*

O may thy soldiers, faithful, true and bold,
fight as the Saints who nobly fought of old,
and win, with them, the victor's crown of gold. *Alleluya!*

O blest communion! fellowship divine!
We feebly struggle, they in glory shine;
yet all are one in thee, for all are thine. *Alleluya!*

The golden evening brightens in the west;
soon, soon to faithful warriors cometh rest:
sweet is the calm of Paradise the blest. *Alleluya!*

From earth's wide bounds, from ocean's farthest coast,
through gates of pearl streams in the countless host,
singing to Father, Son and Holy Ghost. *Alleluya!*

WILLIAM WALSHAM HOW
Ralph Vaughan Williams: 'Sine nomine'

Glorious things of thee are spoken,
 Zion, city of our God;
He whose word cannot be broken
 Form'd thee for his own abode.
On the rock of ages founded,
 What can shake thy sure repose?
With Salvation's walls surrounded,
 Thou may'st smile at all thy foes.

See, the streams of living waters,
 Springing from eternal love,
Well supply thy sons and daughters,
 And all fear of want remove.
Who can faint while such a river
 Ever flows their thirst to assuage;
Grace, which like the Lord the Giver,
 Never fails from age to age?

Round each habitation hovering,
 See the cloud of fire appear,
For a glory and a covering,
 Showing that the Lord is near,
Thus they march, the pillar leading,
 Light by night and shade by day;
Daily on the manna feeding
 Which he gives them when they pray.

Saviour, since of Zion's city
 I, through grace, a member am,
Let the world deride or pity,
 I will glory in Thy Name.

Fading is the world's best pleasure,
   All its boasted pomp and show;
Solid joys and lasting treasure
   None but Zion's children know.

JOHN NEWTON
Franz Joseph Haydn: 'Austria'

God is working his purpose out as year succeeds to year,
God is working his purpose out and the time is drawing near;
Nearer and nearer draws the time, the time that shall surely be,
When the earth shall be filled with the glory of God as the waters
   cover the sea.

What can we do to work God's work, to prosper and increase
The brotherhood of all mankind, the reign of the Prince of Peace?
What can we do to hasten the time, the time that shall surely be,
When the earth shall be filled with the glory of God as the waters
   cover the sea?

March we forth in the strength of God with the banner of Christ
   unfurled,
That the light of the glorious Gospel of truth may shine
   throughout the world.
Fight we the fight with sorrow and sin, to set their captives free,
That the earth may be filled with the glory of God as the waters
   cover the sea.

All we can do is nothing worth unless God blesses the deed;
Vainly we hope for the harvest-tide till God gives life to the seed;
Yet nearer and nearer draws the time, the time that shall surely be,
When the earth shall be filled with the glory of God as the waters
   cover the sea.

ARTHUR CAMPBELL AINGER
Martin Shaw: 'Purpose'

Let all mortal flesh keep silence,
 And with fear and trembling stand;
Ponder nothing earthly-minded,
 For with blessing in his hand
Christ our God to earth descendeth
 Our full homage to demand.

King of kings, yet born of Mary,
 As of old on earth he stood,
Lord of Lords, in human vesture –
 In the Body and the Blood –
He will give to all the faithful
 His own self for heavenly Food.

Rank on rank the host of heaven
 Spreads its vanguard on the way,
As the Light of light descendeth
 From the realms of endless day,
That the powers of hell may vanish
 As the darkness clears away.

At his feet the six-winged Seraph:
 Cherubim with sleepless eye,
Veil their faces to the Presence,
 As with ceaseless voice they cry,
'Alleluia! Alleluia!
 'Alleluia! Lord most high.'

GERARD MOULTRIE
French carol melody: 'Picardy'

Mine eyes have seen the glory of the coming of the Lord;
He is trampling out the vintage where the grapes of wrath are stored;
He hath loosed the fateful lightning of his terrible swift sword;
His truth is marching on.

 Glory! Glory! Hallelujah! Glory! Glory! Hallelujah!
 Glory! Glory! Hallelujah! Our God is marching on!

I have seen him in the watch-fires of a hundred circling camps;
They have builded him an altar in the evening dews and damps;
I have read his righteous sentence by the dim and flaring lamps:
His Day is marching on.

    Glory! Glory! Hallelujah! . . .

I have read a fiery gospel, writ in burnished rows of steel:
'As ye deal with my contemners, so with you my grace shall deal';
Let the Hero born of woman crush the serpent with his heel,
Since God is marching on.

    Glory! Glory! Hallelujah! . . .

He has sounded forth the trumpet that shall never call retreat;
He is sifting out the hearts of men before his judgement seat;
O be swift, my soul, to answer him; be jubilant my feet!
Our God is marching on.

    Glory! Glory! Hallelujah! . . .

In the beauty of the lilies Christ was born across the sea,
With a glory in his bosom that transfigures you and me;
As he died to make men holy, let us die to make men free,
While God is marching on.

    Glory! Glory! Hallelujah! . . .

He is coming like the glory of the morning on the wave;
He is wisdom to the mighty, he is succour to the brave;
So the world shall be his footstool, and the soul of time his slave,
Our God is marching on.

    Glory! Glory! Hallelujah! . . .

JULIA WARD HOWE
Attributed to William Steffe: 'John Brown's Body'

✹

Now thank we all our God,
With heart, and hands, and voices,
Who wondrous things hath done.
In Whom His world rejoices;

Who from our mother's arms
   Hath bless'd us on our way
With countless gifts of love,
   And still is ours to-day.

O may this bounteous God
Through all our life be near us,
   With ever joyful hearts
And blessed peace to cheer us;
   And keep us in His grace,
     And guide us when perplex'd,
And free us from all ills
   In this world and the next.

All praise and thanks to God
The Father now be given,
   The Son, and Him Who reigns
With Them in highest Heaven,
   The One Eternal God,
     Whom earth and Heav'n adore,
For thus it was, is now,
   And shall be evermore. Amen.

MARTIN RINKART
tr. Catherine Winkworth
J. Crüger: 'Nun Danket'

O Thou who camest from above
   The fire celestial to impart,
Kindle a flame of sacred love
   On the mean altar of my heart.

There let it for thy glory burn
   With inextinguishable blaze,
And trembling to its source return
   In humble prayer and fervent praise.

Jesus, confirm my heart's desire
   To work and speak and think for thee;
Still let me guard the holy fire
   And still stir up the gift in me.

Still let me prove thy perfect will,
  My acts of faith and love repeat;
Till death thy endless mercies seal,
  And make the sacrifice complete.

CHARLES WESLEY
Samuel Sebastian Wesley: 'Hereford'

O worship the King all glorious above;
O gratefully sing his power and his love;
Our shield and defender, the Ancient of Days,
Pavilioned in splendour and girded with praise.

O tell of his might, O sing of his grace,
Whose robe is the light, whose canopy space;
His chariots of wrath the deep thunder clouds form,
And dark is his path on the wings of the storm.

The earth with its store of wonders untold,
Almighty, thy power hath founded of old;
Hath stablished it fast by a changeless decree,
And round it hath cast, like a mantle, the sea.

Thy bountiful care what tongue can recite?
It breathes in the air, it shines in the light;
It streams from the hills, it descends to the plain,
And sweetly distils in the dew and the rain.

Frail children of dust and feeble as frail,
In thee do we trust, nor find thee to fail;
Thy mercies how tender, how firm to the end!
Our maker, defender, redeemer, and friend.

O measureless might, ineffable love,
While angels delight to hymn thee above,
Thy humbler creation, though feeble their lays,
With true adoration shall sing to thy praise.

ROBERT GRANT
Psalm 104
William Croft: 'Hanover'

Father, hear the prayer we offer:
　　Not for ease that prayer shall be,
But for strength that we may ever
　　Live our lives courageously.

Not for ever in green pastures
　　Do we ask our way to be;
But the steep and rugged pathway
　　May we tread rejoicingly.

Not for ever by still waters
　　Would we idly rest and stay;
But would smite the living fountains
　　From the rocks along our way.

Be our strength in hours of weakness,
　　In our wanderings be our guide;
Through endeavour, failure, danger,
　　Father, be thou at our side.

L.M. WILLIS
English traditional melody: 'Sussex'

My song is love unknown,
　My saviour's love to me,
Love to the loveless shown,
　That they might lovely be.
　　O who am I,
　　That for my sake
　My Lord should take
　Frail flesh, and die?

He came from his blest throne,
　Salvation to bestow;
But men made strange, and none
The longed-for Christ would know.
　　But O, my Friend,
　　My Friend indeed,
　Who at my need
　His life did spend!

Sometimes they strew his way,
And his sweet praises sing;
Resounding all the day
Hosannas to their King.
Then 'Crucify!'
Is all their breath,
And for his death
They thirst and cry.

Here might I stay and sing.
No story so divine;
Never was love, dear King,
Never was grief like thine!
This is my Friend,
In whose sweet praise
I all my days
Could gladly spend.

SAMUEL CROSSMAN
John Ireland: 'Love Unknown'

Praise to the Holiest in the height,
And in the depth be praise:
In all his words most wonderful,
Most sure in all his ways.

O loving wisdom of our God!
When all was sin and shame,
A second Adam to the fight
And to the rescue came.

O wisest love! that flesh and blood,
Which did in Adam fail,
Should strive afresh against the foe,
Should strive and should prevail;

O generous love! that he, who smote
In Man for man the foe,
The double agony in Man
For man should undergo;

And in the garden secretly,
And on the Cross on high,
Should teach his brethren, and inspire
To suffer, and to die.

Praise to the Holiest in the height,
And in the depth be praise:
In all his words most wonderful,
Most sure in all his ways.

JOHN HENRY NEWMAN
Thomas Haweis: 'Richmond'

Thine be the glory, risen conquering Son,
Endless is the victory thou o'er death hast won;
Angels in bright raiment rolled the stone away,
Kept the folded grave-clothes where the body lay.
Thine be the glory, risen conquering Son,
Endless is the victory thou o'er death hast won.

Lo, Jesus meets us, risen from the tomb;
Lovingly he greets us, scatters fear and gloom;
Let the Church with gladness hymns of triumph sing,
For her Lord now liveth, death hath lost its sting:

No more we doubt thee, glorious Prince of Life;
Life is nought without thee: aid us in our strife;
Make us more than conquerors through thy deathless love;
Bring us safe through Jordan to thy home above.

EDMOND L. BUDRY
tr. Richard Hoyle
George Frideric Handel: 'Maccabaeus'

When I survey the wondrous Cross,
On which the Prince of glory died,
My richest gain I count but loss,
And pour contempt on all my pride.

Forbid it, Lord, that I should boast,
 Save in the death of Christ my God;
All the vain things that charm me most,
 I sacrifice them to his Blood.

See from his head, his hands, his feet,
 Sorrow and love flow mingled down;
Did e'er such love and sorrow meet,
 Or thorns compose so rich a crown?

His dying crimson like a robe,
 Spreads o'er his body on the Tree;
Then am I dead to all the globe,
 And all the globe is dead to me.

Were the whole realm of nature mine,
 That were a present far too small;
Love so amazing, so divine,
 Demands my soul, my life, my all.

ISAAC WATTS
Edward Miller: 'Rockingham'

All people that on earth do dwell,
 Sing to the Lord with cheerful voice;
Him serve with fear, his praise forth tell,
 Come ye before him, and rejoice.

The Lord, ye know, is God indeed;
 Without our aid he did us make;
We are his folk, he doth us feed,
 And for his sheep he doth us take.

O enter then his gates with praise,
 Approach with joy his courts unto;
Praise, laud, and bless his name always,
 For it is seemly so to do.

For why? the Lord our God is good;
   His mercy is for ever sure;
His truth at all times firmly stood,
   And shall from age to age endure.

To Father, Son, and Holy Ghost,
   The God whom heaven and earth adore,
From men and from the angel-host
   Be praise and glory evermore.

WILLIAM KETHE
Louis Bourgeois: 'Old Hundredth'
Arr. Ralph Vaughan Williams

Breathe on me, Breath of God,
   Fill me with life anew,
That I may love what thou dost love,
   And do what thou wouldst do.

Breathe on me, Breath of God,
   Until my heart is pure,
Until with thee I will one will,
   To do and to endure.

Breathe on me, Breath of God,
   Till I am wholly thine,
Until this earthly part of me
   Glows with the fire divine.

Breathe on me, Breath of God,
   So shall I never die,
But live with thee the perfect life
   Of thine eternity.

EDWIN HATCH
Charles Lockhart: 'Carlisle'

Bright the vision that delighted
    Once the sight of Judah's seer;
Sweet the countless tongues united
    To entrance the prophet's ear.

Round the Lord in glory seated
    Cherubim and seraphim
Filled his temple, and repeated
    Each to each the alternate hymn:

'Lord, thy glory fills the heaven;
    Earth is with its fulness stored;
Unto thee be glory given,
    Holy, holy, holy, Lord.'

Heaven is still with glory ringing,
    Earth takes up the angels' cry,
'Holy, holy, holy,' singing,
    'Lord of hosts, the Lord most high.'

With his seraph train before him,
    With his holy Church below,
Thus unite we to adore him,
    Bid we thus our anthem flow:

'Lord, thy glory fills the heaven;
    Earth is with its fulness stored;
Unto thee be glory given,
    Holy, holy, holy, Lord.'

RICHARD MANT
Richard Redhead: 'Laus Deo'

❧

God is Love: let heav'n adore him;
    God is Love: let earth rejoice;
let creation sing before him,
    and exalt him with one voice.
He who laid the earth's foundation,
    he who spread the heav'ns above,
he who breathes through all creation,
    he is Love, eternal Love.

God is Love: and he enfoldeth
    all the world in one embrace;
with unfailing grasp he holdeth
    every child of every race.
And when human hearts are breaking
    under sorrow's iron rod,
then they find that selfsame aching
    deep within the heart of God.

God is Love: and though with blindness
    sin afflicts the souls of men,
God's eternal loving-kindness
    holds and guides them even then.
Sin and death and hell shall never
    o'er us final triumph gain;
God is Love, so Love for ever
    o'er the universe must reign.

TIMOTHY REES
Rowland Huw Pritchard: 'Hyfrydol'

Great is Your faithfulness, O God my Father.
You have fulfilled all Your promise to me.
You never fail and Your love is unchanging.
All you have been You forever will be.

Chorus:
Great is Your faithfulness.
Great is Your faithfulness.
Morning by morning new mercies I see.
All I have needed Your hand has provided.
Great is Your faithfulness, Father, to me.

Summer and winter and springtime and harvest;
Sun, moon and stars in their courses above
Join with all nature in eloquent witness
To your great faithfulness, mercy and love.

Chorus

[133]

Pardon for sin and a peace everlasting,
Your living presence to cheer and to guide,
Strength for today and bright hope for tomorrow;
These are the blessings your love will provide.

Chorus

❧

Holy, holy, holy! Lord God Almighty!
    early in the morning our song shall rise to thee;
holy, holy, holy! merciful and mighty!
    God in three Persons, blessed Trinity!

Holy, holy, holy! all the saints adore thee,
    casting down their golden crowns around the glassy sea;
cherubim and seraphim falling down before thee,
    which wert and art and evermore shalt be.

Holy, holy, holy! though the darkness hide thee,
    though the eye of sinful man thy glory may not see,
only thou art holy, there is none beside thee
    perfect in power, in love, and purity.

Holy, holy, holy! Lord God Almighty!
    all thy works shall praise thy name in earth and sky and sea;
holy, holy, holy! merciful and mighty!
    God in three Persons, blessed Trinity!

REGINALD HEBER
John Bacchus Dykes: 'Nicaea'

❧

How sweet the name of Jesus sounds
In a believer's ear!
It soothes his sorrows, heals his wounds,
And drives away his fear.

It makes the wounded spirit whole,
And calms the troubled breast;
'Tis manna to the hungry soul,
And to the weary rest.

Dear name! the rock on which I build,
My shield and hiding-place,
My never-failing treasury, filled
With boundless stores of grace.

Jesus! my shepherd, brother, friend,
My prophet, priest and king;
My lord, my life, my way, my end,
Accept the praise I bring.

Weak is the effort of my heart,
And cold my warmest thought;
But when I see Thee as Thou art,
I'll praise Thee as I ought.

Till then I would Thy love proclaim
With every fleeting breath;
And may the music of Thy name
Refresh my soul in death!

JOHN NEWTON
Alexander Robert Reinagle: 'St Peter'

Jesus lives! thy terrors now
 Can, O Death, no more appal us;
Jesus lives! by this we know
 Thou, O grave, canst not enthral us.
Alleluya!

Jesus lives! henceforth is death
 But the gate of life immortal;
This shall calm our trembling breath,
 When we pass its gloomy portal.
Alleluya!

Jesus lives! for us he died;
 Then, alone to Jesus living,
Pure in heart may we abide,
 Glory to our Saviour giving.
Alleluya!

[135]

Jesus lives! our hearts know well
   Nought from us his love shall sever;
Life, nor death, nor powers of hell
   Tear us from his keeping ever.
               Alleluya!

Jesus lives! to him the throne
   Over all the world is given;
May we go where he is gone,
   Rest and reign with him in heaven.
               Alleluya!

CHRISTIAN FURCHTEGOTT GELLERT
tr. by Frances Elizabeth Cox
Henry John Gauntlett: 'St Albinus'

Jesu, Lover of my soul,
   Let me to thy bosom fly,
While the nearer waters roll,
   While the tempest still is high:
Hide me, O my Saviour, hide,
   Till the storm of life is past;
Safe into the haven guide,
   O receive my soul at last.

Other refuge have I none;
   Hangs my helpless soul on thee;
Leave, ah! leave me not alone,
   Still support and comfort me.
All my trust on thee is stayed,
   All my help from thee I bring;
Cover my defenceless head
   With the shadow of thy wing.

Thou, O Christ, art all I want;
   More than all in thee I find:
Raise the fallen, cheer the faint,
   Heal the sick, and lead the blind.
Just and holy is thy name;
   I am all unrighteousness;
False and full of sin I am,
   Thou art full of truth and grace.

Plenteous grace with thee is found,
  Grace to cover all my sin;
Let the healing streams abound;
  Make and keep me pure within.
Thou of life the fountain art;
  Freely let me take of thee;
Spring thou up within my heart,
  Rise to all eternity.

CHARLES WESLEY
Joseph Parry: 'Aberystwyth'

Just as I am, without one plea
But that Thy blood was shed for me,
And that Thou bidd'st me come to Thee,
  O Lamb of God, I come.

Just as I am, and waiting not
To rid my soul of one dark blot,
To Thee, whose blood can cleanse each spot,
  O Lamb of God, I come.

Just as I am, though tossed about
With many a conflict, many a doubt,
Fightings and fears within, without,
  O Lamb of God, I come.

Just as I am, poor, wretched, blind;
Sight, riches, healing of the mind,
Yea, all I need, in Thee to find,
  O Lamb of God, I come.

Just as I am, Thou wilt receive,
Wilt welcome, pardon, cleanse, relieve;
Because Thy promise I believe,
  O Lamb of God, I come.

Just as I am – Thy love unknown
Has broken every barrier down –
Now to be Thine, yea, Thine alone,
  O Lamb of God, I come.

Just as I am, of that free love
The breadth, length, depth, and height to prove,
Here for a season, then above, –
    O Lamb of God, I come.

                    CHARLOTTE ELLIOTT
        Arthur Henry Brown: 'Saffron Walden'

Judge eternal, throned in splendour,
    Lord of lords, and King of kings,
with thy living fire of judgement
    purge this realm of bitter things:
solace all its wide dominion
    with the healing of thy wings.

Still the weary folk are pining
    for the hour that brings release:
and the city's crowded clangour
    cries aloud for sin to cease;
and the homesteads and the woodlands
    plead in silence for their peace.

Crown, O God, thine own endeavour;
    cleave our darkness with thy sword;
feed the faithless and the hungry
    with the richness of thy word:
cleanse the body of this nation
    through the glory of the Lord.

                    HENRY SCOTT HOLLAND
Musical Relicks of Welsh Bards: Melody from Edward Jones's 'Rhuddlan'

Lead us, heavenly Father, lead us
O'er the world's tempestuous sea;
Guard us, guide us, keep us, feed us
For we have no help but thee;
Yet possessing every blessing,
If our God our Father be.

Saviour, breathe forgiveness o'er us:
All our weakness thou dost know;
Thou didst tread this earth before us,
Thou didst feel its keenest woe;
Lone and dreary, faint and weary,
Through the desert thou didst go.

Spirit of our God, descending,
Fill our hearts with heavenly joy,
Love with every passion blending,
Pleasure that can never cloy:
Thus provided, pardoned, guided,
Nothing can our peace destroy.

JAMES EDMESTON
Thomas Binney, from Friedrich Filitz: 'Mannheim'

Light's abode, celestial Salem,
  Vision whence true peace doth spring,
Brighter than the heart can fancy,
  Mansion of the highest King;
O how glorious are the praises
  Which of thee the prophets sing!

There for ever and for ever
  Alleluia is outpoured;
For unending, for unbroken
  Is the feast-day of the Lord;
All is pure and all is holy
  That within thy walls is stored.

There no cloud or passing vapour
  Dims the brightness of the air;
Endless noon-day, glorious noon-day,
  From the Sun of suns is there;
There no night brings rest from labour,
  For unknown are toil and care.

O how glorious and resplendent,
  Fragile body, shalt thou be,
When endued with so much beauty,

Full of health and strong and free,
Full of vigour, full of pleasure
That shall last eternally.

Now with gladness, now with courage,
Bear the burden on thee laid,
That hereafter these thy labours
May with endless gifts be paid;
And in everlasting glory
Thou with brightness be arrayed.

Laud and honour to the Father,
Laud and honour to the Son,
Laud and honour to the Spirit,
Ever Three and ever One,
Consubstantial, co-eternal,
While unending ages run.

THOMAS À KEMPIS
tr. J. M. Neale
Henry Smart: 'Regent Square'

Lord, bring the day to pass
when forest, rock and hill,
the beasts, the birds, the grass,
will know your finished will:
when we attain our destiny
and nature its lost unity.

Forgive our careless use
of water, ore and soil;
the plenty we abuse,
supplied by others' toil:
save us from making self our creed,
turn us towards our neighbour's need.

Give us, when we release
creation's secret powers,
to harness them for peace,
our children's peace and ours:
teach us the art of mastering,
which makes life rich and draws death's sting.

Creation groans, travails,
bound in its futile plight
until the hour it hails
the new found of the light,
who enter on their true estate.
Come, Lord: new heavens and earth create.

Lord of beauty, thine the splendour
    Shown in earth and sky and sea,
Burning sun and moonlight tender,
    Hill and river, flower and tree:
Lest we fail our praise to render
    Touch our eyes that they may see.

Lord of wisdom, whom obeying
    Mighty waters ebb and flow,
While unhasting, undelaying,
    Planets on their courses go:
In thy laws thyself displaying,
    Teach our minds thyself to know.

Lord of life, alone sustaining
    All below and all above,
Lord of love, by whose ordaining
    Sun and stars sublimely move:
In our earthly spirits reigning,
    Lift our hearts that we may love.

Lord of beauty, bid us own thee,
    Lord of truth, our footsteps guide,
Till as Love our hearts enthrone thee,
    And, with wisdom purified,
Lord of all, when all have known thee,
    Thou in all art glorified.

CYRIL ARGENTINE ALINGTON
Henry Smart: 'Regent Square'

Love divine, all loves excelling,
  Joy of heav'n, to earth come down,
Fix in us thy humble dwelling,
  All thy faithful mercies crown.
Jesu, thou art all compassion,
  Pure unbounded love thou art;
Visit us with thy salvation,
  Enter every trembling heart.

Breathe, O breathe thy loving spirit
  Into every troubled breast!
Let us all in thee inherit,
  Let us find that second rest.
Take away our bent to sinning,
  Alpha and Omega be;
End of faith, as its beginning.
  Set our hearts at liberty.

Come, almighty to deliver,
  Let us all thy life receive;
Suddenly return, and never,
  Never more thy temples leave.
Thee we would be always blessing,
  Serve thee as thy hosts above,
Pray, and praise thee, without ceasing,
  Glory in thy perfect love.

Finish then thy new creation,
  Pure and sinless let us be;
Let us see thy great salvation,
  Perfectly restored in thee:
Changed from glory into glory,
  Till in heav'n we take our place,
Till we cast our crowns before thee,
  Lost in wonder, love, and praise!

CHARLES WESLEY
Rowland Huw Pritchard: 'Hyfrydol'

O Day of God, draw nigh
   in beauty and in power,
come with thy timeless judgement now
   to match our present hour.

Bring to our troubled minds,
   uncertain and afraid,
the quiet of a steadfast faith,
   calm of a call obeyed.

Bring justice to our land,
   that all may dwell secure,
and finely build for days to come
   foundations that endure.

Bring to our world of strife
   thy sovereign word of peace,
that war may haunt the earth no more
   and desolation cease.

O Day of God, draw nigh;
   as at creation's birth
let there be light again, and set
   thy judgements in the earth.

R.B.Y. SCOTT
Adapted from Anglo-Genevan Psalms: 'St Michael'

O Lord my God! when I in awesome wonder
Consider all the works Thy hand hath made.
I see the stars, I hear the mighty thunder,
Thy pow'r throughout the universe displayed:

Chorus:
Then sings my soul, my Saviour God, to thee,
How great Thou art! How great Thou art!
Then sings my soul, my Saviour God, to thee,
How great Thou art! How great Thou art!

[143]

When through the woods and forest glades I wander
And hear the birds sing sweetly in the trees;
When I look down from lofty mountain grandeur,
And hear the brook, and feel the gentle breeze;

And when I think that God His Son not sparing,
Sent Him to die – I scarce can take it in.
That on the cross my burden gladly bearing,
He bled and died to take away my sin;

When Christ shall come with shout of acclamation
And take me home – what joy shall fill my heart!
Then shall I bow in humble adoration
And there proclaim, my God, how great Thou art!

O praise ye the Lord! praise him in the height;
Rejoice in his word, ye angels of light;
Ye heavens adore him by whom ye were made,
And worship before him, in brightness arrayed.

O praise ye the Lord! praise him upon earth,
In tuneful accord, ye sons of new birth;
Praise him who hath brought you his grace from above,
Praise him who hath taught you to sing of his love.

O praise ye the Lord, all things that give sound;
Each jubilant chord re-echo around;
Loud organs, his glory forth tell in deep tone,
And, sweet harp, the story of what he hath done.

O praise ye the Lord! thanksgiving and song
To him be outpoured all ages along;
For love in creation, for heaven restored,
For grace of salvation, O praise ye the Lord! Amen.

HENRY WILLIAMS BAKER
Psalms 148 and 150
Charles Hubert Parry: 'Laudate Domino'

O valiant Hearts, who to your glory came
Through dust of conflict and through battle-flame;
Tranquil you lie, your knightly virtue proved.
Your memory hallowed in the Land you loved.

Proudly you gathered, rank on rank to war,
As who had heard God's message from afar;
All you had hoped for, all you had, you gave
To save Mankind – yourselves you scorned to save.

Splendid you passed, the great surrender made,
Into the light that nevermore shall fade;
Deep your contentment in that blest abode,
Who wait the last clear trumpet-call of God.

Long years ago, as earth lay dark and still,
Rose a loud cry upon a lonely hill,
While in the frailty of our human clay
Christ, our Redeemer, passed the self-same way.

Still stands His Cross from that dread hour to this
Like some bright star above the dark abyss;
Still, through the veil, the Victor's pitying eyes
Look down to bless our lesser Calvaries.

These were His servants, in His steps they trod,
Following through death the martyr'd Son of God:
Victor He rose; victorious too shall rise
They who have drunk His cup of Sacrifice.

O risen Lord, O Shepherd of our Dead,
Whose Cross has brought them and those whose Staff has led –
In glorious hope their proud and sorrowing Land
Commits her Children to Thy gracious hand.

SIR JOHN S. ARKWRIGHT

O worship the Lord in the beauty of holiness,
   Bow down before him, his glory proclaim;
With gold of obedience and incense of lowliness,
   Kneel and adore him: the Lord is his name.

Low at his feet lay thy burden of carefulness,
High on his heart he will bear it for thee,
Comfort thy sorrows, and answer thy prayerfulness,
Guiding thy steps as may best for thee be.

Fear not to enter his courts in the slenderness
Of the poor wealth thou wouldst reckon as thine;
Truth in its beauty, and love in its tenderness,
These are the offerings to lay on his shrine.

These, though we bring them in trembling and fearfulness,
He will accept for the name that is dear;
Mornings of joy give for evenings of tearfulness,
Trust for our trembling, and hope for our fear.

O worship the Lord in the beauty of holiness,
   Bow down before him, his glory proclaim;
With gold of obedience and incense of lowliness,
   Kneel and adore him: the Lord is his name.

JOHN SAMUEL BEWLEY MONSELL
'Was Lebet, was Schwebet'

Praise Him on the trumpet,
   the psaltery and harp;
Praise Him on the timbrel
   and the dance;
Praise Him with stringed
   instruments too;
Praise Him with the loud cymbals;
Praise Him with the loud cymbals;
Let everything that has breath
Praise the Lord!

Alleluia – praise the Lord;
Alleluia – praise the Lord;
Let everything that has breath
Praise the Lord!

Alleluia – praise the Lord;
Alleluia – praise the Lord;
Let everything that has breath
Praise the Lord!

☙

Praise to the Lord, the Almighty, the King of creation;
O my soul, praise Him, for He is thy health and salvation;
All ye who hear,
Now to His temple draw near,
Joining in glad adoration.

Praise to the Lord, Who o'er all things so wondrously reigneth,
Shieldeth thee gently from harm, or when fainting sustaineth:
Has thou not seen
How thy heart's wishes have been
Granted in what He ordaineth?

Praise to the Lord, Who doth prosper thy work and defend thee,
Surely His goodness and mercy shall daily attend thee;
Ponder anew
What the Almighty can do,
If to the end He befriend thee. Amen.

JOACHIM NEANDER
tr. Catherine Winkworth
'Hast du denn, Jesu'

☙

Sunset and evening star,
And one clear call for me!
And may there be no moaning of the bar,
When I put out to sea,

But such a tide as, moving, seems asleep,
Too full for sound and foam,
When that which drew from out the boundless deep
Turns again home.

Twilight and evening bell,
And after that the dark!
And may there be no sadness of farewell,
When I embark;
For, though from out our bourne of time and place
The flood may bear me far, . . .
I hope to see my Pilot face to face
When I have crost the bar.
Amen.

ALFRED, LORD TENNYSON
Joseph Barnby: 'Crossing the Bar'

The spacious firmament on high,
With all the blue ethereal sky,
And spangled heav'ns, a shining frame,
Their great Original proclaim.
The unwearied sun from day to day
Does his Creator's power display,
And publishes to every land
The work of an almighty hand.

Soon as the evening shades prevail
The moon takes up the wondrous tale,
And nightly to the list'ning earth
Repeats the story of her birth;
Whilst all the stars that round her burn,
And all the planets in their turn,
Confirm the tidings, as they roll,
And spread the truth from pole to pole.

What though, in solemn silence, all
Move round the dark terrestrial ball?
What though nor real voice nor sound
Amid their radiant orbs be found?

In reason's ear they all rejoice,
And utter forth a glorious voice,
For ever singing, as they shine,
'The hand that made us is divine.'

JOSEPH ADDISON
Psalm 19
Henry Walford Davies: 'Firmament'

There is a green hill far away,
  Without a city wall,
Where the dear Lord was crucified,
  Who died to save us all.

We may not know, we cannot tell,
  What pains he had to bear,
But we believe it was for us
  He hung and suffered there.

He died that we might be forgiven,
  He died to make us good,
That we might go at last to heaven,
  Saved by his precious Blood.

There was no other good enough
  To pay the price of sin;
He only could unlock the gate
  Of heaven, and let us in.

O dearly, dearly has he loved,
  And we must love him too,
And trust in his redeeming Blood,
  And try his works to do.

MRS ALEXANDER
William Horsley: 'Horsley'

Ye holy angels bright,
  Who wait at God's right hand,
Or through the realms of light
  Fly at your Lord's command,
    Assist our song,
      Or else the theme
      Too high doth seem
    For mortal tongue.

Ye blessèd souls at rest,
  Who ran this earthly race,
And now, from sin released,
  Behold the Saviour's face,
    His praises sound,
      As in his sight
      With sweet delight
    Ye do abound.

Ye saints, who toil below,
  Adore your heavenly King,
And onward as ye go
  Some joyful anthem sing;
    Take what he gives,
      And praise him still
      Through good and ill,
    Who ever lives.

My soul, bear thou thy part,
  Triumph in God above,
And with a well-tuned heart
  Sing thou the songs of love.
    Let all thy days
      Till life shall end,
      Whate'er he send,
    Be filled with praise.

JOHN HAMPDEN GURNEY
John Darwall: 'Darwall's 148th'

Sung Music

PIE JESU

from *Requiem*

Pie Jesu Domine
Dona eis requiem

Pie Jesu Domine
Dona eis requiem sempiternam requiem

Pie Jesu Domine
Dona eis sempiternam requiem

GABRIEL FAURÉ

LIBERA ME

from *Requiem*

Libera me, Domine de morte aeterna
In die illa tremenda
Quando coeli movendi sunt et terra
Dum veneris judicare saeculum per ignem.

Tremens factus sum ego
Et timeo,
Dum discussio venerit atque ventura ira

Dies illa
Dies irae
Calamitatis,
Et miseriae
Dies illa,
Dies magna
Et amara valde
Requiem aeternam
Dona eis Domine
Et lux perpetua luceat eis

Libera me Domine de morte aeterna
In die illa tremenda
Quando coeli movendi sunt et terra,
Dum veneris judicare saeculum per ignem.

Libera me Domine,
Libera me Domine.

GABRIEL FAURÉ

IN PARADISUM

from *Requiem*

In paradisum deducant Angeli: in tuo adventu suscipiant te Martyres, et perducant te in civitatem sanctam Jerusalem. Chorus Angelorum te suscipiat, et cum Lazaro quondam paupere aeternam habeas requiem.

May the angels lead you into Paradise; at your coming may the martyrs receive you and lead you into the holy city Jerusalem. May the Choir of Angels receive you, and with Lazarus who once was poor may you have eternal rest.

GABRIEL FAURÉ

GOD BE IN MY HEAD

God be in my head,
and in my understanding;

God be in mine eyes,
and in my looking;

God be in my mouth,
and in my speaking;

God be in my heart,
and in my thinking;

God be at mine end,
and at my departing.

HENRY WALFORD DAVIES

Bring us, O Lord God, at our last awakening into the house and gate
of heaven, to enter into that gate and dwell in that house, where
there shall be no darkness nor dazzling but one equal light, no noise
nor silence, but one equal music, no fears nor hopes but one equal
possession, no ends nor beginnings but one equal eternity, in the
habitation of thy glory and dominion, world without end. Amen.

WILLIAM HARRIS
John Donne

NUNC DIMITTIS

Lord, now lettest thou thy servant depart in peace, according to thy
  word.
For mine eyes have seen thy salvation,
Which thou hast prepared before the face of all people;
To be a light to lighten the Gentiles, and to be the glory of thy people
  Israel.

Glory be to the Father, and to the Son, and to the Holy Ghost;
As it was in the beginning, is now, and ever shall be, world without
  end. Amen.

WILLIAM BYRD

THE STAR-SPANGLED BANNER

Oh, say can you see, by the dawn's early light,
  What so proudly we hailed at the twilight's last gleaming,
Whose broad stripes and bright stars thro' the perilous fight,
  O'er the ramparts we watched were so gallantly streaming?

[155]

And the rocket's red glare, the bombs bursting in air,
Gave proof thro' the night that our flag was still there.
Oh, say, does that star-spangled banner yet wave
O'er the land of the free and the home of the brave?

JOHN STAFFORD SMITH

THE NATIONAL ANTHEM

God save our gracious Queen!
Long live our noble Queen!
 God save the Queen!
Send her victorious,
Happy and glorious,
Long to reign over us;
 God save the Queen!

WE WAIT FOR THY LOVING KINDNESS

We wait for thy loving kindness, O God; in the midst of the temple:
 Alleluya.
O God, according to thy name, so is thy praise unto the world's end.
Thy right hand full of righteousness: Alleluya.

WILLIAM MCKIE

Words selected by the Revd C.M. Armitage

PIE JESU

from *Requiem*

Pie Jesu, qui tollis peccata mundi: dona eis requiem
Agnus Dei, qui tollis peccata mundi: dona eis requiem, dona eis
requiem sempiternam requiem.

ANDREW LLOYD WEBBER

VASKRES IZ GROBA

Being risen from the tomb, having burst the bonds of Hell, Thou, O Lord, hast loosened condemnation of death, delivering all from the snares of the enemy.

SERGEY RACHMANINOV

SEVENFOLD AMEN

JOHN STAINER

I'M IN LOVE WITH THE WORLD

I'm in love with the world, with its fires and its seas and its pain. I'm in love with the world, as it spins round my soul again.

JO COLLINS

PSALM 55

O for the wings of a dove!
Far away, far away would I rove;
In the wilderness build me a nest,
And remain there for ever at rest.

FELIX MENDELSSOHN

from MESSIAH

I know that my redeemer liveth, and that he shall stand at the latter day upon the earth; and though worms destroy this body, yet in my flesh shall I see God. For now is Christ risen from the dead, the first-fruits of them that sleep.

GEORGE FRIDERIC HANDEL

Faire is the heaven where happy soules have place
In full enjoyment of felicitie;
Whence they doe still behold the glorious face
Of the Divine Eternall Majestie.

Yet farre more faire be those bright Cherubins,
Which all with golden wings are overdight,
And those eternal burning Seraphins,
Which from their faces dart out fierie light;
Yet fairer than they both, and much more bright
Be th' Angels and Archangels, which attend
On God's owne person without rest or end.

These then in faire each other farre excelling,
As to the Highest they approch more neare,
Yet is that Highest farre beyond all telling,
Fairer than all the rest which there appeare;
Though all their beauties joynd together were:
How then can mortall tongue hope to expresse
The image of such endless perfectnesse?

WILLIAM HARRIS
Edmund Spenser

PSALM 121

I will lift up mine eyes unto the hills, from whence cometh my help.
My help cometh even from the Lord, who hath made heaven and
earth.
He will not suffer thy foot to be moved, and he that keepeth thee will
not sleep.
Behold, he that keepeth Israel shall neither slumber nor sleep.
The Lord himself is thy keeper; the Lord is thy defence upon thy right
hand;
So that the sun shall not burn thee by day neither the moon by night.
The Lord shall preserve thee from all evil, yea, it is even he that shall
keep thy soul.
The Lord shall preserve thy going out, and thy coming in from this
time forth for evermore.

Glory be to the Father, and to the Son, and to the Holy Ghost;
As it was in the beginning, is now, and ever shall be world without
end. Amen.

WILLIAM MCKIE

PSALM 121

Lift thine eyes to the mountains, whence cometh help.
Thy help cometh from the Lord, the Maker of heaven and earth.
He hath said, Thy foot shall not be moved: thy keeper will never slumber.

FELIX MENDELSSOHN

from REVELATION

And I saw a new heaven and a new earth: for the first heaven and the
first earth were passed away; and there was no more sea.

And I John saw the holy city, new Jerusalem, coming down from God
out of heaven, prepared as a bride adorned for her husband.

And I heard a great voice out of heaven saying, Behold, the tabernacle
of God is with men, and he will dwell with them, and they shall be his
people, and God himself shall be with them, and be their God.

And God shall wipe away all tears from their eyes; and there shall be no
more death, neither sorrow, nor crying, neither shall there be any more
pain: for the former things are passed away.

EDGAR BAINTON

KYRIE

from *Mass in C minor*

WOLFGANG AMADEUS MOZART

KYRIE

from *Mass No. 2 in E minor*

Kyrie eleison
Christe eleison
Kyrie eleison

ANTON BRUCKNER

from SONG OF SOLOMON

Set me as a seal

Set me as a seal upon thine heart,
As a seal upon thine arm:
For love is strong as death;
Many waters cannot quench love,
Neither can the floods drown it;
Set me as a seal upon thine heart
For love is strong as death.

WILLIAM WALTON

AVE MARIA

from *The Well-Tempered Clavier*

Father Almighty,
Lord, we adore Thee,
Bending before Thee!
Hear us, unworthy tho' we be,
Thy love is never failing,
Over all prevailing,
Bounteous is Thy mercy, and Thy grace is ever free.
Father, O hear us!
Father, O hear us!
O hear us!

While we bow before Thee,
Humbly we adore Thee,
Hear us O Hear us, and let Thy blessing rest on us!
Amen!

Adapted by CHARLES GOUNOD from J.S. BACH

HOW LOVELY ARE THY DWELLINGS

from *Requiem*

How lovely are Thy dwellings fair, O Lord of Hosts,
My soul longeth, yea, longeth and fainteth for the courts of
   the Lord; my heart and flesh ring out their joy unto the living God.
How lovely are Thy dwellings fair, O Lord of Hosts.
Blessed are they, yea, blessed, blessed are they that dwell in Thy house:
   they praise Thee, Lord, evermore.
How lovely are Thy dwellings fair.

JOHANNES BRAHMS

EVENING HYMN

Thee, Lord, before the close of day,
Maker of all things, thee we pray
For thy dear loving kindness' sake
To guard and guide us in thy way.

Banish the dreams that terrify,
And night's fantastic company:
Keep us from Satan's tyranny:
Defend us from unchastity.

Protect us, Father, God adored,
Thou too, co-equal Son and Lord,
Thou, Holy Ghost, our Advocate,
Whose reign can know nor bound nor date.

BALFOUR GARDINER

BLESS THE LORD

from *Song of the Three Children*

Bless the Lord the God of our fathers:
  sing his praise and exalt him for ever.
Bless his holy and glorious name:
  sing his praise and exalt him for ever.
Bless him in his holy and glorious temple:
  sing his praise and exalt him for ever.
Bless him who beholds the depths:
  sing his praise and exalt him for ever.
Bless him who sits between the cherubim:
  sing his praise and exalt him for ever.
Bless him on the throne of his kingdom:
  sing his praise and exalt him for ever.
Bless him in the heights of heaven:
  sing his praise and exalt him for ever.
Bless the Father the Son and the Holy Spirit:
  sing his praise and exalt him for ever.

CHANT BY C.F. SOUTH

from THE PEARL FISHERS

Au fond du temple saint paré de fleurs et d'or
Une femme apparaît
Je crois la voir encore
La foule prosternée
La regarde étonnée
Et murmure tout bas
Voyez c'est la déesse
Qui dans l'ombre se dresse
Et vers nous tend les bras
Son voile se soulève
O vision! O rêve!

La foule est à genoux
Oui, c'est elle,
C'est la déesse plus charmante et plus belle,
Oui, c'est elle, c'est la déesse qui descend parmi nous
Son voile se soulève
Et la foule est à genoux.

Mais à travers la foule elle s'ouvre un passage
Son long voile déjà nous cache son visage
Mon regard hélas
La cherche en vain

Elle fuit!
Elle fuit!

Mais dans mon âme soudain
Quelle étrange ardeur s'allume
Quel feu nouveau me consume
Ta main repousse ma main
Ta main repousse ma main
De nos coeurs l'amour s'empare
Et nous change en ennemis.
Non, que rien ne nous sépare,
Non rien! que ne nous sépare,
Jurons de rester amis,
Jurons de rester amis,
Oh! oui, jurons de rester amis!

Oui, c'est elle,
C'est la déesse
En ce jour qui vient nous unir
Et fidèle à ma promesse,
Comme un frère je veux te chérir!
C'est elle, c'est la déesse
Qui vient en ce jour nous unir!
Oui, partageons le même sort,
Soyons unis jusqu'à la mort!

The holy temple gleamed with garlands richly set
And a woman appeared
I think I see her yet
The crowd that knelt in prayer gazed at her sitting there

And they whispered and said
Behold!
It is the goddess!
There she stands in the shadows with her pale arms outspread
The veil she wore was lifted – Ah!
She was fair as Heaven
The people all bowed their heads.
Night of wonder!
Yes, 'tis the goddess.
Holy, fair and enchanting,
Bless the goddess come down among us
Bless the earth where she treads!
Ah, now the veil was lifted
And the people bowed their heads

She turned towards the people and they made way before her.
She was veiled then and so her lovely face was hidden
Though I gazed
Alas! I gazed in vain

She was gone!
She was gone!

But she had captured my soul
And my heart was yearning for her
A sudden fire burned within me
I spurned the hand of a friend
I spurned the hand of a friend
And this love turned me against you.
We were now changed into foes
No! Let nothing more divide us,
Nothing!
Let nothing more divide us,
Nothing!
We swear we are friends till death
We swear we are friends till death!

So this promise made to each other
Shall our faithful hearts unite ever more
Brother to brother
Nothing now can break the faith we plight
Ah, truly that was the goddess came to us upon that magic night

So will we share all Fate can send
What e'er may be till life shall end.

GEORGES BIZET

from MESSIAH

The trumpet shall sound, and the dead shall be raised incorruptible, and
we shall be changed. For this corruptible must put on incorruption, and
this mortal must put on immortality.

GEORGE FRIDERIC HANDEL

STABAT MATER

Pro peccatis suae gentis
Vidit Jesum in tormentis
El flagellis subditum:
Vidit suum dulcem natum
Morientem desolatum
Dum emisit spiritum.

GIOACCHINO ROSSINI

ES IST EIN ROESS ENTSPRUNGEN

Es ist ein Roess entsprungen
aus einer Wurzel zart,
als uns die Alten sungen,
aus Jesse kam die Art
und hat ein Blümlein bracht
mitten im kalten Winter,
wol zu der halben Nacht.

Das Rosslein, das ich meine,
darvon Esaias sagt,
hat uns gebracht alleine

Mary die reine Magd
aus Gottes ewgem Raht
hat sie ein Kind gebohren
bleibend ein reine Magd.

Das Blümelein so kleine,
das duftet uns so suss;
mit seinem hellen Scheine
vertreibts die Finsternis;
wahr Mensch und wahrer Gott,
hilft uns aus allem Leide,
rettet von Sünd und Tod.

Of Jesse's line descended
By ancient sibyls sung,
with thornless branch extended,
From noble root new-sprung,
A rose doth bear a flower,
All in the cold mid-winter
And at the midnight hour.

That flower of ancient splendour,
Of which Isaiah spake,
Mary, the rose-branch tender,
Puts forth, for mankind's sake;
Obedient to God's will
A little child she bears us,
Yet is a maiden still.

The frozen air perfuming,
That tiny bloom doth swell;
Its rays, the night illuming,
The darkness quite dispels.
O Rose beyond compare,
Bloom in our hearts' mid-winter;
Restore the springtime there!

MICHAEL PRAETORIUS

HERZLICH TUT MICH VERLANGEN

Erscheine mir zum Schilde
zum Trost in meinem Tod
und lass mich sehn dein Bilde
in deiner Kreuzesnot.

Da will ich nach dir blikken
da will ich glaubensvoll
dich fest an mein Herz drükken,
wer so stirbt, der stirbt wohl.

Wenn ich einmal soll scheiden
so scheide nicht von mir
Wenn ich den Tod soll leiden
so tritt du dann herfur.

Wenn mir am aller bängsten
wird um das Herze sein
dann reiss mich aus den Ängstenkraft
deiner Angst und Pein.

SIGFRID KARG-ELERT

IF YE LOVE ME

If ye love me, keep my commandments, and I will pray the Father, and
he shall give you another Comforter, that he may abide with you for
ever, even the Spirit of truth.

THOMAS TALLIS

PANIS ANGELICUS

O Lord of mercy,
O Lord of justice,
Thine own and humble servants seek to find redemption with
infinite wisdom.

Thou dost look on us,
Saviour, Saviour,
Thou art miraculous,
Saviour, Saviour,
We would Thy servants be.

Singing our praise to Thee,
To Thee our hearts do flee,
Glorious Thy name shall be until eternity.
E'en in the silent night,
Thy glory shining bright,
Proclaims to mortals Thy ever glorious might
Father of men
To Thee we bring our song of praise.

CÉSAR FRANCK

IN DIR IST FREUDE

In dir ist Freude in allem Leide,
o du süsser Jesu Christ;
durch dich wir haben himmlische Gaben,
der du wahrer Heiland bist.
Hilfest von Schanden,
rettest von Banden; wer dir vertrautet hat wohl gebauet,
wird ewig bleiben
Halleluja!
Zu deiner Güte steht unser G'müte,
an dir wir kleben im Tod und Leben;
nichts kann uns scheiden
Halleluja!

In Thee is gladness
Amid all sadness,
Jesus, Sunshine of my heart!
By Thee are given
The gifts of Heaven,
Thou the true Redeemer art!
Our souls Thou wakest, our bonds Thou breakest,
Who trusts Thee surely hath built securely,
He stands for ever: Hallelujah!

Our hearts are pining to see Thy shining,
Dying or living to Thee are cleaving,
Nought can us sever: Hallelujah!

J. S BACH
Johann Lindemann, tr. C. Winkworth

ANTHEMS FOR THE CORONATION OF GEORGE II

The King Shall Rejoice

The King shall rejoice in Thy strength, O Lord;
Exceeding glad shall he be of Thy salvation;
Glory and great worship hast Thou laid upon him.
Thou hast prevented him with the blessings of goodness
and hast set a crown of pure gold upon his head.
Alleluja! Amen.

Zadok the Priest

Zadok, the priest and Nathan, the prophet, anointed Solomon, King, –
And all the people rejoiced and said,
God save the King, long live the King, may
the King live for ever!
Amen. Alleluja!

My Heart is Inditing

My heart is inditing of a good matter; I speak of
the things which I have made unto the King.
Kings' daughters were among thy honourable women.
Upon thy right hand did stand the Queen in vesture of gold,
and the King shall have pleasure in thy beauty.
Kings shall be thy nursing fathers, and
Queen thy nursing mothers.

Let Thy Hand be Strengthened

Let thy hand be strengthened, and thy right
hand be exalted.
Let justice and judgement be the preparation
of thy seat; let mercy and truth go before thy face.
Alleluja.

GEORGE FRIDERIC HANDEL

PSALM 46

God is our hope and strength, a very present help in trouble.
Therefore will we not fear, though the earth be moved, and though
the hills be carried into the midst of the sea.
Though the waters thereof rage and swell, and though the mountains
shake at the tempest of the same.
The rivers of the flood thereof shall make glad the city of God, the
holy place of the tabernacle of the most Highest.
God is in the midst of her, therefore shall she not be removed: God
shall help her, and that right early.
The heathen make much ado, and the kingdoms are moved: but
God hath shewed his voice, and the earth shall melt away.
The Lord of hosts is with us: the God of Jacob is our refuge.
O come hither, and behold the works of the Lord, what destruction
he hath brought upon the earth.
He maketh wars to cease in all the world: he breaketh the bow, and
knappeth the spear in sunder, and burneth the chariots in the fire.
Be still then, and know that I am God: I will be exalted among the
heathen, and I will be exalted in the earth.
The Lord of hosts is with us: the God of Jacob is our refuge.
Glory be to the Father, and to the Son, and to the Holy Ghost;
As it was in the beginning, is now, and ever shall be, world without
end. Amen.

HYMN OF PRAISE

I waited for the Lord, He inclined unto me. He heard my complaint.
O blessed are they that hope and trust in the Lord.

FELIX MENDELSSOHN

Come you not from Newcastle,
Come you not there away?
O met you not my true love,
Riding on a bonny bay?

Why should I not love my love?
Why should not my love love me?
Why should I not speed after him,
Since love to all is free?

TRADITIONAL

ANTHEM

Thou wilt keep him in perfect peace, whose mind is stayed on thee. The darkness is no darkness with thee, but the night is as clear as the day; the darkness and light to thee are both alike. God is light, and in Him is no darkness at all. O let my soul live, and it shall praise thee. For thine is the Kingdom, the power, and the glory, for evermore. Thou wilt keep him in perfect peace, whose mind is stayed on thee.

SAMUEL SEBASTIAN WESLEY

I heard a voice from heaven, saying unto me, Write, from henceforth blessed are the dead which die in the Lord; even so saith the Spirit; for they rest from their labours.

JOHN GOSS

HAVE MERCY, LORD

from *St Matthew Passion*

Have mercy, Lord, on me, regard my bitter weeping.
Look on me, Heart and eyes both weep to Thee,
weep to Thee bitterly.
Have mercy, Lord on me.

JOHANN SEBASTIAN BACH

WALKING IN THE AIR

from *The Snowman*

We're walking in the air, we're floating in the moonlit sky;
the people far below are sleeping as we fly.
I'm holding very tight, I'm riding in the midnight blue,
I'm finding I can fly so high above with you.

Children gaze open-mouthed, taken by surprise;
nobody down below believes their eyes.
We're walking in the air, we're dancing in the midnight sky,
and everyone who sees us greets us as we fly.

HOWARD BLAKE

AMAZING GRACE

Amazing grace! how sweet the sound
    That saved a wretch like me!
I once was lost, but now am found,
    Was blind, but now I see.

'Twas grace that taught my heart to fear,
    And grace my fears relieved;
How precious did that grace appear
    The hour I first believed.

Through many dangers, toils, and snares
    I have already come;
'Tis grace hath brought me safe thus far,
    And grace will lead me home.

The Lord has promised good to me,
    His word my hope secures;
He will my shield and portion be
    As long as life endures.

JOHN NEWTON

GLORIA

from *Henry VIII*

Gloria in excelsis Deo, et in terra pax hominibus bonae voluntatis.

Glory be to God on high, and in earth peace, good will towards men.

GUY WOOLFENDEN

PSALM 117

Laudate Dominum omnes gentes: laudate eum omnes populi.
Quoniam confirmata est super nos misericordia eius: et veritas
Domini manet in aeternum.
Gloria Patri et Filio et Spiritui Sancto; sicut erat in principio et nunc
et semper et in saecula saeculorum. Amen.

O Praise the Lord, all ye heathen: praise him, all ye nations.
For his merciful kindness is ever more and more towards us: and the truth
of the Lord endureth for ever.
Glory be to the Father, and to the Son: and to the Holy Ghost;
As it was in the beginning, is now, and ever shall be: world without
end. Amen.

WOLFGANG AMADEUS MOZART

PSALM 150

O praise God in his holiness: praise him in the firmament of his power.
Praise him in his noble acts: praise him according to his excellent
greatness.
Praise him in the sound of the trumpet: praise him upon the lute
and harp.
Praise him in the cymbals and dances: praise him upon the strings
and pipe.
Praise him upon the well-tuned cymbals: praise him upon the loud
cymbals.

Let every thing that hath breath praise the Lord.
Glory be to the Father, and to the Son, and to the Holy Ghost;
As it was in the beginning, is now, and ever shall be, world without
end. Amen.

CHARLES VILLIERS STANFORD

PSALM 119

Beati quorum via integra est: qui ambulant in lege Domini.

*Blessed are those that are undefiled in the way: and walk in the law of the
Lord.*

CHARLES VILLIERS STANFORD

LANCAN LI JORN

When the days are long in May,
I'm leased by the sweet songs of the birds from afar;
and when that I have turned away,
I remember a love from afar.
I go, without longing, sombre and bowed down,
so that neither song nor white-thorn blossom
avails me more than icy winter.

The Lord indeed I hold as true
through whom I'll see that love from afar;
but, for one good that it all befalls me,
I have two ills, since I'm so far,
Ah! why am I not a pilgrim there,
so that my staff and my cloak
were beheld by her lovely eyes.

JAUFFRE RUDEL DE BLAYE

AVE VERUM CORPUS

Ave verum corpus, natum de Maria Virgine
vere passum immolatum in cruce pro homine.
Cujus latus perforatum unda fluxit sanguine.
Esto nobis praegustatum in mortis examine,
O dulcis, O pie, O Jesu Fili Mariae,
miserere me. Amen.

Hail, true body, born of the blessed Virgin,
which to redeem us suffered in anguish upon
the cross: from whose side, when pierced by
the spear, there came forth both water and
blood; be to us at our last hour the source
of consolation. O sweet, O loving, thou Son
of Mary, have mercy upon me. Amen.

WILLIAM BYRD

God is gone up with a triumphant shout
The Lord with sounding trumpets' melodies.
Sing praises out, sing praises out.
Unto our King sing praise seraphic-wise!
Lift up your heads ye lasting Doors, they sing,
And let the King of Glory enter in.
Methinks I see Heaven's sparkling courtiers fly
In flocks of Glory down him to attend.
And hear Heart-cramping notes of Melody
Surrounding his Chariot as it did ascend;
Mixing their music, making ev'ry string
More to enravish as they this tune sing.

GERALD FINZI
Edward Taylor

PSALM 104

O Lord, how manifold are thy works: in wisdom hast thou made
them all; the earth is full of thy riches.

So is the great and wide sea also: wherein are things creeping
innumerable, both small and great beasts.

There go the ships, and there is that Leviathan: whom thou hast made
to take his pastime therein.

These wait all upon thee: that thou mayest give them meat in due
season.

When thou givest it them they gather it: and when thou openest thy
hand they are filled with good.

When thou hidest thy face they are troubled: when thou takest away
their breath they die, and are turned again to their dust.

When thou lettest thy breath go forth they shall be made: and thou
shalt renew the face of the earth.

The glorious majesty of the Lord shall endure for ever: the Lord shall
rejoice in his works.

The earth shall tremble at the look of him: if he do but touch the hills,
they shall smoke.

I will sing unto the Lord as long as I live: I will praise my God while I
have my being.

And so shall my words please him: my joy shall be in the Lord.

As for sinners, they shall be consumed out of the earth, and the
ungodly shall come to an end: praise thou the Lord, O my soul,
praise the Lord.

Glory be to the Father, and to the Son: and to the Holy Ghost;

As it was in the beginning, is now, and ever shall be: world without
end. Amen.

from THE CREATION

Achieved is the glorious work; our song let be the praise of God.
Glory to his name for ever. He sole on high exalted reigns.
Hallelujah.

FRANZ JOSEPH HAYDN

PSALMS 5 AND 4

Lead me, Lord, lead me in thy righteousness: make thy way plain
  before my face.
For it is thou, Lord, only that makest me dwell in safety.

SAMUEL SEBASTIAN WESLEY

from PSALM 34

O taste and see how gracious the Lord is: blest is the man that trusteth
in him.

RALPH VAUGHAN WILLIAMS

PSALM 15

Lord, who shall dwell in thy tabernacle: or who shall rest upon thy
  holy hill?
Even he that leadeth an uncorrupt life, and doeth the thing which is
  right, and speaketh the truth from his heart.
He that hath used no deceit in his tongue, nor done evil to his
  neighbour, and hath not slandered his neighbour.
He that setteth not by himself, but is lowly in his own eyes, and
  maketh much of them that fear the Lord.
He that sweareth unto his neighbour, and disappointeth him not,
  though it were to his own hindrance.
He that hath not given his money upon usury, nor taken reward
  against the innocent.
Whoso doeth these things shall never fall.
Glory be to the Father, and to the Son, and to the Holy Ghost;
As it was in the beginning, is now, and ever shall be, world without
  end. Amen.

from THE PILGRIM'S PROGRESS

After this it was noised abroad that Mr Valiant-for-Truth was taken with a summons, and had this for a token that the summons was true, *That his pitcher was broken at the fountain.* When he understood it, he called for his friends, and told them of it. Then said he, 'I am going to my fathers, and though with great difficulty I am got hither, yet now I do not repent me of all the trouble I have been at to arrive where I am. My sword, I give to him that shall succeed me in my pilgrimage, and my courage and skill, to him that can get it. My marks and scars I carry with me, to be a witness for me that I have fought his battles who now will be my rewarder.'

When the day that he must go hence was come, many accompanied him to the River side, into which, as he went, he said, '*Death, where is thy sting?*' and as he went down deeper, he said, '*Grave, where is thy victory?*'

So he passed over, and all the trumpets sounded for him on the other side.

RALPH VAUGHAN WILLIAMS
John Bunyan

Christ be with me, Christ within me,
Christ behind me, Christ before me,
Christ beside me, Christ to win me,
Christ to comfort and restore me,
Christ beneath me, Christ above me,
Christ in quiet, Christ in danger,
Christ in hearts of all that love me,
Christ in mouth of friend and stranger.

arranged by CHARLES VILLIERS STANFORD
St Patrick

Watch, watch and pray, Jesus will keep to his word.

IONA COMMUNITY

BE NEAR ME, LORD, WHEN DYING

from *St Matthew Passion*

Be near me, Lord, when dying
O part not thou from me,
And to my succour flying,
Come Lord and set me free.
And when my heart must languish
In death's last awful throe
Release me from my anguish
By thine own pain and woe.

JOHANN SEBASTIAN BACH
arr. by William Cole

NUNC DIMITTIS

Lord, now lettest thou thy servant depart in peace, according to thy
   word.
For mine eyes have seen, thy salvation,
Which thou hast prepared, before the face of all people,
To be a light to lighten the Gentiles, and to be the glory of thy people
   Israel.
Glory be to the Father, and to the Son, and to the Holy Ghost;
As it was in the beginning, is now, and ever shall be, world without
   end. Amen.

The Book of Common Prayer

SANCTUS

from *Requiem*

Sanctus, Sanctus, Sanctus, Dominus Deus Sabaoth.
Pleni sunt coeli et terra gloria tua.
Hosanna in excelsis.

Holy, Holy, Holy, Lord God of hosts.
Heaven and earth are full of thy glory, O Lord.
Hosanna in the highest.

GABRIEL FAURÉ

THREEFOLD AMEN

ORLANDO GIBBONS

RING OF BRIGHT WATER

Where sun and the wind play on a ring of bright water,
That's where my heart land will be.
The deer on the hill, and the first snow of winter,
The gull in the sky winging free.
I wandered away from the dark crowded city
Leaving my old life behind,
And came to a place where a ring of bright water
Dazzled the care from my mind.
So, I live with the wonder of the sky and the sea;
And I'll always remember who revealed them to me.
But now you are gone with your whirlpools of laughter
Racing me down to the sea;
But I'll always smile when a ring of bright water
Echoes your laughter to me.
It echoes your laughter to me.

FRANK CORDELL
Betty Botley

ELISABETH'S GREETING

from *Tannhäuser*

Dich, teure Halle, grüss' ich wieder,
Froh grüss' ich dich, geliebter Raum!
In dir erwachen seine Lieder,
Und wecken mich aus düstrem Traum.

Da er aus dir geschieden,
Wie öd' erschienst du mir!
Aus mir entfloh der Frieden,
Die Freude zog aus dir.
Wie jetzt mein Busen hoch sich hebet,

So scheinst du jetzt mir stolz und hehr.
Der dich und mich so neu belebet,
Nicht länger weilt er ferne mehr.
Wie jetzt mein Busen hoch sich hebet, etc.
Sei mir gegrüsst! sei mir gegrüsst!

Dear hall, I greet thee once again
joyfully I greet thee, beloved place!
In thee his lays awake
and waken me from gloomy dreams.

When he departed from thee,
how desolate thou didst appear to me!
Peace forsook me,
joy took leave of thee.
How strongly now my heart is leaping;

to me now thou dost appear exalted and sublime.
He who thus revives both me and thee,
tarries afar no more.
How strongly now by heart is leaping, etc.
I greet thee! I greet thee!

RICHARD WAGNER

EASTER HYMN

from *Cavalleria Rusticana*

Church Choir
Regina coeli laetare,
Quia, quem meruisti portare,
Resurrexit sicut dixit.

Villagers
Alleluia!

Inneggiamo, il Signor non è morto!
Ei fulgente ha dischiuso l'avel.
Inneggiamo al Signore risorto,
oggi asceso alla gloria del ciel.
Inneggiamo, il Signor non è morto, etc.

Santuzza
Inneggiamo, il Signor non è morto,
inneggiamo, al Signore risorto,
oggi asceso alla gloria del ciel.

Villagers
Alla gloria del ciel.

Choir
Alleluia!

Church Choir
Rejoice, O Queen of heaven,
because He whom thou wast found worthy to bear
has risen from the dead as He said He would.

Villagers
Alleluia!
Let us give praise, Our Lord is not dead.
Shining in glory He has opened the tomb.
Let us give praise to the risen Lord,
ascended this day to the glory of Heaven.
Let us give praise, Our Lord is not dead, etc.

Santuzza
Let us give praise, Our Lord is not dead,
let us give praise to the risen Lord,
ascended this day to the glory of Heaven.

Villagers
To the glory of Heaven.

Choir
Alleluia!

PIETRO MASCAGNI

INGEMISCO

from *Requiem*

Ingemisco tamquam reus:
Culpa rubet vultus meus:
Supplicanti parce, Deus.
Qui Mariam absolvisti,
Et latronem exaudisti,
Mihi quoque spem dedisti.
Preces meae non sunt dignae:
Sed tu, bonus, fac benigne,
Ne peranni cremer igne.
Inter oves locum praesta,
Et ab haedis me sequestra,
Statuens in parte dextra.

I groan as one guilty:
and my face blushes with guilt:
spare the suppliant, O God.
Thou who didst absolve Mary (Magdalen)
and heard the prayer of the thief,
hast given me hope too.
My prayers are not worthy,
but Thou, O good one, show mercy,
lest I burn in everlasting fire.
Give me a place among the sheep,
and separate me from the goats,
placing me on Thy right hand.

GIUSEPPE VERDI

VA PENSIERO

from *Nabucco*

Chorus of Hebrews
Va, pensiero, sull'ali dorate;
va, ti posa sui clivi, sui colli,
ove olezzano tepide e molli

l'aure dolci del suolo natal!
Del Giordano le rive saluta
di Sionne le torri atterrate . . .
Oh, mia patria si bella a perduta!
Oh, membranza si cara e fatal!

Arpa d'or dei fatidici vati,
perche muta dal salice pendi?

Le memorie nel petto raccendi,
ci favella del tempo che fu!
O simile di Solima ai fati
traggi un suono di crudo lamento,
o t'inspiri il Signore un concento
che ne infonda al patire virtu!

Fly, thought, on wings of gold;
go settle upon the slopes and the hills,
where, soft and mild, the sweet airs
of our native land smell fragrant!
Greet the banks of Jordan
and Zion's toppled towers . . .
Oh, my country so lovely and lost!
Oh, remembrance so dear and fraught with despair!
Golden harp of the prophetic seers,
why dost thou hang mute upon the willow?
Re-kindle our memories,
and speak of times gone by!
Mindful of the fate of Jerusalem,
give forth an air of sad lamentation,
or else let the Lord imbue us
with fortitude to bear our sufferings!

GIUSEPPE VERDI

IN QUESTA REGGIA

from *Turandot*

Turandot
In questa reggia, or son mill'annie mille un grido disperato risonò,
E quel grido, traverso stirpe e stirpe quì nell'anima mia si refugiò.
Principessa Lo-u-Ling, ava dolce e serena che regnavi nel tuo cupo
    silenzio in gioja pura,
e sfidasti inflessibile e sicura l'aspro dominio,
oggi rivivi in me!

Chorus
Fu quando il Re dei Tartari le sette sue bandiere dispiegò.

Turandot
Pure nel tempo che ciascun ricorda,
fusgomento e terore e rombo d'armi!
Il regno vinto!
Il regno vinto!
E Lo-u-Ling la mia ava trascinata
da un uomo, come te, come te
straniero, là nella notte atroce,
dove si spense la sua fresca voce!

Chorus
Da secoli ella dorme nella
sua tomba enorme.

Turandot
O Principi, che a lunghe carovane
d'ogni parte del mondo qui venite a gettar la vostra sorte,
io vendico su voi,
su voi quella purezza,
quel grido e quella morte!
Quel grido e quella morte!
Mai nessun m'avrà
Mai nessun, nessun m'avrà!
L'orror di chi l'uccise
vivo nel cor mista!
No, no! Mai nessun m'avrà!

Ah, rinasce in me
l'orgoglio ditanta purità!
Straniero! Non tentar la fortuna!
Gli enigmi sono tre, la morte è una!

Prince
No! No! Gli enigmi sono tre,
una è la vita!

Turandot
No! No! Gli enigmi sono tre,
la morte è una!

Turandot
Within this palace, a thousand thousand years ago a cry of tortur'd anguish rent the air,
Cry of anguish, that, trav'lling down the ages, in my heart has, at last found a resting place.
Noble Princess Lo-u-Ling, thou example of wisdom who did'st rule in strict seclusion and glory o'er thy people,
and defying with firm unyielding will the rule of man,
thou livest still in me!

Chorus
'Twas when the King of Tartary display'd his seven red and hostile flags!

Turandot
Yet in those days as ev'ryone remembers,
war broke out with the clash of arms and terror!
Her realm was conquer'd!
Her realm was conquer'd!
And Lo-u-Ling, noble Princess, roughly captur'd
by a man, a man like thee, like thee
O stranger, cruelly dragg'd to torture,
till her imploring voice was still for ever!

Chorus
For ages without number,
She sleeps in her great tomb.

Turandot
Ye Princes who, in caravans and splendour,

from the four corners of the world come hither intent to try your fortune,
I will avenge on you,
who broke that lily,
that agonizing cry!
That cry that dying cry!
Ne'er shall I be wed!
Ne'er shall man possess me!
The hate of him who kill'd her
lives in my heart fore'er!
Never mortal man!
Ah! I ne'er will betray
the glory of such chastity!
Then stranger! Do not challenge thy fortune!
The riddles are three, there is one death!

Prince
No! No! The riddles are three,
there is one life!

Turandot
No! No! The riddles are three,
there is one death!

GIACOMO PUCCINI

Justorum animae in manu Dei sunt, et non tanget illos
tormentum malitiae.
Visi sunt oculis insipientium mori: illi autem sunt in pace.

The souls of the righteous are in the hand of God, and there shall no
torment touch them.
In the sight of the unwise they seemed to die: but they are in peace.

CHARLES VILLIERS STANFORD

DIDO'S LAMENT

from *Dido and Aeneas*

When I am laid in earth, may my wrongs create
  No trouble in thy breast.
Remember me! but ah! forget my fate.

HENRY PURCELL

from MASS IN G

Agnus Dei,
qui tollis peccata mundi,
miserere nobis;

Agnus Dei,
qui tollis peccata mundi,
miserere nobis;

Agnus Dei,
qui tollis peccata mundi,
dona nobis pacem.

O Lamb of God,
that takest away the sins of the world,
have mercy upon us.

O Lamb of God,
that takest away the sins of the world,
have mercy upon us.

O Lamb of God,
that takest away the sins of the world,
grant us thy peace.

FRANCIS POULENC

ABOUT YOUTH

from *The Song of the Earth*

Mitten in dem kleinen Teiche
Steht ein Pavillon aus grünem
Und aus weissem Porzellan.

Wie der Rücken eines Tigers
Wölbt die Brücke sich aus Jade
Zu dem Pavillon hinüber.

In dem Häuschen sitzen Freunde,
Schön gekleidet, trinken, plaudern,
Manche schreiben Verse nieder.

Ihre seidnen Ärmel gleiten
Rückwärts, ihre seidnen Mützen
Hocken lustig tief im Nacken.

Auf des kleinen Teiches stiller
Wasserfläche zeigt sich alles
Wunderlich im Spiegelbilde.

Alles auf dem Kopfe stehend
In dem Pavillon aus grünem
Und aus weissem Porzellan;

Wie ein Halbmond scheint die Brücke,
Umgekehrt der Bogen. Freunde,
Schön gekleidet, trinken, plaudern.

In the middle of the little pond
Stands a pavilion of green
And white porcelain.

Like the back of a tiger
The bridge of jade arches
Across to the pavilion.

In the little house friends are sitting,
Beautifully dressed, drinking, chattering;
Some are writing down verses.

Their silken sleeves glide
Back, their silken caps
Perch cheerfully on the backs of their heads.

On the little pond's still
Surface everything is seen
Curiously mirrored.

They are all standing on their heads
In the pavilion of green
And white porcelain;

The bridge shines like a half-moon,
Its arch upside-down. Friends,
Beautifully dressed, are drinking, chattering.

GUSTAV MAHLER

from JUBILATE AGNO

Rejoice in God, O ye Tongues; give the glory to the Lord and the
  Lamb.
Nations, and languages, and every Creature, in which is the breath of
  Life.
Let man and beast appear before him, and magnify his name together.
Let Nimrod, the mighty hunter, bind a Leopard to the altar, and
  consecrate his spear to the Lord.
Let Ishmael dedicate a Tyger, and give praise for the liberty in which
  the Lord has let him at large.
Let Balaam appear with an Ass, and bless the Lord his people and his
  creatures for a reward eternal.
Let Daniel come forth with a Lion, and praise God with all his might
  through faith in Christ Jesus.
Let Ithamar minister with a Chamois, and bless the name of Him, that
  cloatheth the naked.
Let Jakem with the Satyr bless God in the dance.
Let David bless with the Bear – the beginning of victory to the Lord –
  to the Lord the perfection of excellence –

Hallelujah from the heart of God and from the hand of the artist
    inimitable, and from the echo of the heavenly harp in sweetness
    magnifical and mighty.

BENJAMIN BRITTEN
Christopher Smart

SIT DOWN, YOU'RE ROCKIN' THE BOAT

from *Guys and Dolls*

I dreamed last night I got on the boat to Heaven
And by some chance I had brought my dice along
And there I stood
And I hollered 'Someone fade me'
But the passengers they know right from wrong.
For the people all said sit down,
Sit down, you're rockin' the boat.
People all said sit down sit down you're rockin' the boat
And the devil will drag you under
By the sharp lapel of your checkered coat
Sit down sit down sit down sit down sit down
You're rockin' the boat

I sailed away on that little boat to Heaven
And by some chance found a bottle in my fist
And there I stood, nicely passin' out the whiskey
But the passengers were bound to resist
For the people all said beware,
You're on a heavenly trip,
People all said beware
Beware you'll scuttle the ship
And the Devil will drag you under
By the fancy tie 'round your wicked throat
Sit down, sit down, sit down, sit down, sit down
You're rockin' the boat

And as I laughed at those passengers to Heaven
A great big wave came and washed me overboard
And as I sank
And I hollered 'Someone save me',

That's the moment I woke up, thank the Lord.
And I said to myself sit down, sit down,
You're rockin' the boat
Said to myself sit down,
Sit down
You're rockin' the boat
And the Devil will drag you under
With a soul so heavy you'd never float,
Sit down sit down sit down sit down, sit down
You're rockin' the boat.

FRANK LOESSER

TONIGHT, TONIGHT

from *West Side Story*

Tonight, tonight
Won't be just any night,
Tonight there will be no morning star.
Tonight, tonight,
I'll see my love tonight.
And for us, stars will stop where they are.

Today
The minutes seem like hours,
The hours go so slowly,
And still the sky is light.
Oh moon, grow bright,
And make this endless day endless night! . . .

We're gonna jazz it tonight
They're gonna get it tonight – tonight.
They began it – they began it
And we're the ones
To stop 'em once and for all!
The Sharks are gonna have their way
The Sharks are gonna have their day
We're gonna rock it tonight –
Tonight!

Tonight,
Late tonight,
We're gonna mix it tonight.
Anita's gonna have her day,
Anita's gonna have her day,
Bernardo's gonna have his way
Tonight – tonight.
Tonight – this very night,
We're gonna rock it tonight!
They began it.
They began it.
We'll stop 'em once and for all!
The Jets are gonna have their way,
The Jets are gonna have their day,
We're gonna rock it tonight.
Tonight!
– Tonight there will be no morning star
Tonight, tonight, I'll see my love tonight
And for us, stars will stop where they are.

Today the minutes seem like hours.
The hours go so slowly,
And still the sky is light.
Oh moon, grow bright,
And make this endless day endless night,
Tonight!

LEONARD BERNSTEIN

THE WIND BENEATH MY WINGS

It must have been cold there in my shadow, to never have sunlight
    on your face.
You've been content to let me shine, you always walked the step
    behind.
I was the one with all the glory, while you were the one with all
    the strength.
Only a face without a name, I never once heard you complain.
Did you ever know that you're my hero, and ev'ry thing I'd
    like to be?

[193]

I can fly higher than an eagle, 'cause you are the wind beneath
    my wings.
It might have appeared to go unnoticed that I've got it all here
    in my heart.
I want you to know the truth: I would be nothing without you.
You are the wind beneath my wings.

LARRY HENLY and JEFF SILBAR

NON, JE NE REGRETTE RIEN

Non! Rien de rien . . .
Non! Je ne regrette rien . . .
Ni le bien, qu'on m'a fait,
Ni le mal, tout ça m'est bien égal!

Non! Rien de rien . . .
Non! Je ne regrette rien . . .
C'est payé, balayé, oublié,
Je me fous du passé!

Avec mes souvenirs
J'ai allumé le feu,
Mes chagrins, mes plaisirs,
Je n'ai plus besoin d'eux!
Balayées les amours,
Et tous leurs trémolos,
Balayés pour toujours
Je repars à zéro.

Car ma vie,
Car mes joies,
Aujourd'hui
Ça commence avec toi.

CHARLES DUMONT
Michael Vaucaire/Irving Taylor

LIFE IS JUST A BOWL OF CHERRIES

From the musical *George White's Scandals* – 11th edition

Life is Just a Bowl of Cherries,
Don't make it serious,
Life's too mysterious,
You work, you save, you worry so,
But you can't take your dough when you go, go, go;
So keep repeating it's the berries
The strongest oak must fall.
The sweet things in life,
To you were just loaned,
So how can you lose what you've never owned.
Life is Just a Bowl of Cherries,
So live and laugh at it all.

LEW BROWN and RAY HENDERSON

EAST ANGLIAN FOLK SONG

What's the life of a man any more than a leaf?
A man has his season so why should he grieve?
Although in this world we appear fine and gay
Like a leaf we must wither and soon fade away.

As I was a-walking one morning in ease,
I viewed all the leaves as they fell from the trees.
All in full motion appearing to be
But those that had withered had fell from the tree.

What's the life of a man any more than a leaf? . . .

If you'd seen the trees but a few days ago
How beautiful and bright did their leaves seem to grow;
A frost came upon them and withered them all;
A storm came among them and down they did fall.

What's the life of a man any more than a leaf? . . .

If you look in a churchyard there you will see
Those that have withered like the leaves on a tree.
When age and affliction upon us doth call,
Like the leaf we must wither and down we must fall.

What's the life of a man any more than a leaf? . . .

What's the life of a man any more than a leaf?
A man has his season, so why should he grieve?
Although in this world we appear fine and gay,
Like the leaf we must wither and soon fade away.

ANON.

EXSULTATE, JUBILATE

from *Motet for Soprano in F Major*

Exsultate
Tu virginum corona
Alleluja, alleluja.

WOLFGANG AMADEUS MOZART

BIBO'S SONG

Bibo is my name and I'm a band
Got a thousand tunes in my hand
And I've played the Coast of Spain, I've been around
And my agent's got me booked
For a winter in Berlin
Or is it Rome . . .?
Bibo is my name and I'm a band.

All I need's a piano and a chair
Doesn't matter much if no one's there
'Cos I've got a big selection I can play
Fit for any clientele
Or any time of night or day
Bibo is my name and I'm a band

Chorus

Find me in a hotel in the spring
Just before the season gets in swing
Pretty soon and I'll be moving on
There's a beat group coming in
And summer people like a different song . . .
Bibo is my name and I'm a band

Chorus

If there's something you would like to hear
Say the name or hum it to me clear
I'll try to play it nice, play it true
And if you come again I'll recall your face
And play it just for you
Bibo is my name and I'm a band . . .

JONATHAN MAGONET

ARISE! YE STARVELINGS

Arise! ye starvelings from your slumbers;
Arise ye criminals of want.
For reason in revolt now thunders.
And ends at last the age of cant.
Now away with all superstitions!
Servile masses, arise! arise!
We'll change forthwith the old conditions
And spurn the dust to win the prize.
    Then comrades, come rally,
    And the last fight let us face.
    The International
    Unites the human race.

OLD RIVERS

How old was I when I first saw Old Rivers?
I can't remember when he wasn't around.
Well, that old fella did a heap of work.
Spent his whole life walkin' ploughed ground.
He had a one-room shack not far from us,
And we was about as poor as him.
He had one old mule called 'Midnight',
And I trailed along after him.

Chorus:
He'd say [now] one of these days
I'm gonna climb that mountain,
Walk up there among them clouds,
Where the cotton's high and the corn's a-growin',
And there ain't no fields to plough.
With the sun beatin' down, 'cross the field I see, that mule, Old
    Rivers and me.

He used to plough them rows straight and deep,
And I'd come along there behind
Bustin' up clods with my own bare feet,
Old Rivers was a friend of mine.
The sun would get high and that mule would work
And Old Rivers would finally say 'whoa!'
He'd wipe his brow and lean back on the reins
And talk about a place he's gonna go.

I got a letter today from the folks back home.
They're all fine and the crops are dry.
Down near the end Mom said,
'Son, you know Old Rivers died.'
Sittin' here now in this new-ploughed earth
Tryin' to find me a little shade,
With the sun beatin' down across the field
I see that mule, Old Rivers, and me.

CLIFF CROFFORD

LEANING ON A LAMP-POST

from Me and My Gal

Leaning on a lamp,
Maybe you think I look a tramp,
Or you may think I'm hanging round to steal a car;
But no, I'm not a crook,
And if you think that's what I look,
I'll tell you why I'm here and what my motives are.

I'm leaning on a lamp-post at the corner of the street,
In case a certain little lady comes by
Oh me, Oh my,
I hope the little lady comes by.
I don't know if she'll get away,
She doesn't always get away,
But anyway I know that she'll try.
Oh me, Oh my,
I hope the little lady comes by.
There's no other girl I could wait for,
But this one I'd break any date for,
I won't have to ask what she's late for,
She'd never leave me flat,
She's not a girl like that,
She's absolutely wonderful and marvellous and beautiful,
And anyone can understand why
I'm leaning on a lamp-post at the corner of the street,
In case a certain little lady comes by.
I'm by.

NOEL GAY

ICH BIN DER WELT ABHANDEN GEKOMMEN /

LOST AM I TO THE WORLD

Ich bin der Welt abhanden gekommen,
mit der ich sonst viele Zeit verdorben;
sie hat so lange nichts von mir vernommen,
sie mag wohl glauben, ich sei gestorben!

Es ist mir auch gar nichts daran gelegen,
ob sie mich für gestorben hält.
Ich kann auch gar nichts sagen dagegen,
denn wirklich bin ich gestorben der Welt.

Ich bin gestorben dem Weltgetümmel
und ruh' in einem stillen Gebiet!
Ich leb' allein in meinem Himmel,
in meinem Lieben, in meinem Lied.

Lost am I to the world,
with which I used to waste much time;
so long has it heard naught of me,
well may it think me dead!

Nor is it to me of consequence
if it should so consider me.
Nor can I say aught against it,
for truly I am dead to the world.

Dead am I to the world's tumult
and rest in a quiet realm!
I live alone in my heaven,
in my love and in my song.

GUSTAV MAHLER
Friedrich Rückert

THE WAITER AND THE PORTER AND THE
UPSTAIRS MAID

from the film *Birth of the Blues*

The people in the ballroom were stuffy and arty,
So I began to get just a little afraid.
I sneaked into the kitchen and found me a party;
The waiter and the porter and the second story maid.

I peeked into the parlor to see what was hatchin',
In time to hear the hostess suggest a charade,
But who was in the pantry a-laughin' and scratchin';
The waiter and the porter and the second story maid.

When they heard the music that the orchestra played,
The waiter and the porter grabbed a-hold of the maid
Then they all proceeded to go into a clog
Hot diggety dog!

If ever I'm invited to some fuddy duddy's
I ain't a-gonna watch any harlequinade,
You'll find me in the kitchen applaudin' my buddies;
The waiter and the porter and the upstairs maid.

JOHNNY MERCER

AVE MARIA

Ave Maria!
O listen to our prayer!
We pray,
O Maria, hear this prayer!
We need Thy blessing this hour so fair.
Bless this love, this heavenly hour so fair,
Bless this hour so fair!
Safe may we sleep beneath Thy care,
And guard this love we so tenderly share!
O Maiden, send your heavenly answer!
O Maiden, hear this fervent pray'r.
Ave Maria!

FRANZ SCHUBERT

AGNUS DEI

Agnus Dei, qui tollis peccata mundi, miserere nobis.
Agnus Dei, qui tollis peccata mundi, dona nobis pacem.

Lamb of God, that takest away the sin of the world, have mercy upon us.
Lamb of God, that takest away the sin of the world, grant us peace.

ORLANDO GIBBONS

GREATER LOVE HATH NO MAN

Many waters cannot quench Love,
neither can floods drown it.
Love is strong as death.
Many waters cannot quench Love.

Greater Love hath no man than this,
that a man lay down his life for his friends.
Who His own Self bare our sins in His own Body on the tree,
that we, being dead to sins, should live unto righteousness.

Ye are washed, ye are sanctified, ye are justified,
in the Name of the Lord Jesus;
Ye are a chosen generation, a royal priesthood, a holy nation,
That ye should shew forth the praises of Him who
call'd you out of darkness, out of darkness into His marvellous light.

I beseech you, brethren, by the mercies of God
that ye present your bodies, a living sacrifice,
holy, holy, acceptable unto God, which is your reasonable service.

JOHN IRELAND

THE LORD BLESS YOU AND KEEP YOU

The Lord bless you and keep you,
the Lord lift his countenance upon you,
and give you peace,
The Lord make his face to shine upon you,
and be gracious unto you.
Amen.

PETER C. LUTKIN
Arranged by Lawrence Grant

from THE CREATION

The heavens are telling the glory of God, the wonder of his work displays the firmament.
Today that is coming speaks it the day, the night that is gone to following night.

In all the lands resounds the word, never unperceived, ever understood.

The heavens are telling the glory of God, the wonder of his work displays the firmament.

FRANZ JOSEPH HAYDN

A SPIRITUAL

from *A Child of our Time*

Deep river, my home is over Jordan,
Lord, I want to cross over into camp ground.

Oh, chillun!
Oh, don't you want to go,
To that gospel feast,
That promised land,
That land where all is peace?

Walk into heaven, and take my seat,
And cast my crown at Jesus' feet,
Lord, I want to cross over into camp ground,
Deep river, my home is over Jordan,
Lord, I want to cross over into camp ground.

MICHAEL TIPPETT

UP WHERE WE BELONG

Who knows what tomorrow brings;
In a world, few hearts survive?
All I know is the way I feel;
When it's real, I keep it alive.
The road is long.
There are mountains in our way,
But we climb a step every day.

Love lift us up where we belong,
Where the eagles cry
On a mountain high.
Love lift us up where we belong,
Far from the world we know;
Up where the clear winds blow.

Some hang on to 'used-to-be',
Live their lives looking behind.
All we have is here and now;
All our life, out there to find.
The road is long.
There are mountains in our way,
But we climb them a step every day.

Love lift us up . . .

Time goes by,
No time to cry,
Life's you and I,
Alive, today.

Love lift us up . . .

Other Music

JOHN ADDISON   *Reach for the Sky* (film)

TOMASO GIOVANNI ALBINONI   Adagio in G minor

GREGORIO ALLEGRI   *Miserere*

MALCOLM ARNOLD   Siciliano (Suite for Brass)

JOHANN SEBASTIAN BACH   Double Concerto for Two Violins: 2nd
movement, largo ma non tanto
Fantasia and Fugue in G minor BWV 542
Prelude and Fugue in G BWV 541
Concerto in A minor: 1st movement, Allegro
Fugue in G minor BWV 1000
'Wachet auf, ruft uns die Stimme' BWV 645
'Have mercy, Lord, on me' from *St Matthew Passion*, BWV 244
'In tears of grief' from *St Matthew Passion*
Toccata and Fugue in D minor BWV 565
Toccata and Fugue in D minor, 'Dorian', BWV 538
Prelude and Fugue 'St Anne' in E flat BWV 552
Prelude in B minor Choral preludes
Prelude in E minor BWV 548
Prelude in C minor BWV 546
Toccata and Fugue in F major BWV 540
Fantasia in G major BWV 572
Passacaglia in C minor BWV 582
'Jesu, joy of man's desiring'
'Lord hear my longing' from *The Wise Virgins*, arr. by William
Walton

LUDWIG VAN BEETHOVEN   Symphony No. 6 in F major 'Pastoral'
3rd movement, Peasants Dancing

LÉON BOËLLMANN   *Suite Gothique*

ALEXANDER PORFIRYEVICH BORODIN   The Steppes of Central Asia

JOHANNES BRAHMS   Adagio, from Clarinet quintet in B minor, op.
115
Double concerto for violin and cello: slow movement

FRANK BRIDGE   Three idylls for string quartet

BENJAMIN BRITTEN   Four Sea Interludes from *Peter Grimes* – Dawn

DIETRICH BUXTEHUDE   'Komm heiliger Geist'
'Ach Herr, mich armen Sünder'

FRÉDÉRIC CHOPIN   Andante spianato in G major from *A Month in
the Country*, arr. Lanchbery
Largo from Cello Sonata in G minor, op. 65

JEREMIAH CLARKE 'Trumpet Voluntary' from *The Prince of Denmark's March* from B.M. add. Ms 31465, transcribed by Sir Henry Wood

FREDERICK DELIUS   Brigg Fair: An English Rhapsody

MARCEL DUPRÉ   Prelude and Fugue in B major

EBB and KANDER   'New York, New York'

EDWARD ELGAR   'Nimrod' from *Enigma* Variations
    Chanson de Matin
    Salut D'Amore
    Allegro maestoso from Sonata in G
    Proficiscere anima Christiana from *The Dream of Gerontius*
    Triumphal March from *Caractacus*
    Sonata in G: 1st movement
    Introduction and Allegro for Strings

CÉSAR FRANCK   Pastorale

ALEXANDER GLAZUNOV   excerpts from *Birthday Offering*

CHRISTOPH WILLIBALD GLUCK   'Dance of the Blessed Spirits' from *Orfeo et Euridice*

BENNY GOODMAN   'Body and Soul'

GAVIN GORDON   'Faithful Girl' from *The Rake's Progress*

GEORGE FRIDERIC HANDEL   *Music for the Royal Fireworks*
    Suite from the *Water Music*

BASIL HARWOOD   Dithyramb, op. 7

FRANZ JOSEPH HAYDN   St Anthony Chorale

GUSTAV HOLST   Movements from *Military Suite*

ALAN HOVHANESS   Prayer of St Gregory

JOSEPH WILCOX JENKINS   Arioso

SIGFRID KARG-ELERT   *Marche Triomphale: Nun Danket Alle Gott*
    'O Gott, du frommer Gott'

ALBERT KETÈLBEY   In a Monastery Garden

CONSTANT LAMBERT   Prelude, Sarabande and other excerpts from *Horoscope*

FRANZ LISZT   'Marguerite and Armand' excerpt from Sonate in B minor

JEAN-BAPTISTE LOEILLET   Gigue-Vivace from Sonata in B flat for Trumpet and Organ

GUSTAV MAHLER   Adagietto from Symphony No. 5
    Symphony No. 5

FELIX MENDELSSOHN   Sonata No. 4 in B flat
    Sonata No. 3 in A, 1st movement

ENNIO MORRICONE   *The Mission*

WOLFGANG AMADEUS MOZART   Piano Concerto in C, K467
     Divertimento, K136
     Fantasia in F Minor
     String quartet in C, K465, 1st movement: Adagio-Allegro
     String quartet in G major, K156
     Fantasia in F minor, K608
     Piano concerto in C, Slow movement
     Movements from Serenade No. 10 in B flat major
JOHANN PACHELBEL   Canon and gigue in D
PARKER   Pieces from *Banana Blush*
FLOR PEETERS   Aria
SERGEY PROKOFIEV   Balcony pas de deux from *Romeo and Juliet*
GIACOMO PUCCINI   Chrysanthemums
HENRY PURCELL   Voluntary on the Old 100th
     'Sound the Trumpet'
SERGEY RACHMANINOV   Rhapsody on a Theme of Paganini
MAURICE RAVEL   Pavane pour une infante défunte
     Piano Concerto in G major (Adagio assai)
RICHARD RODGERS   Waltz from *Carousel*
ERIK SATIE   *Gymnopédies*
FRANZ SCHUBERT   String quartet in G major, Op. 161, Andante
     String quintet in C major, Adagio
     'Notturno', Piano Trio in E flat
ROBERT SCHUMANN   Piano Concerto in A minor
HENRY SMART   Andante No. 1 in A
JOHN STANLEY   Trumpet Tune
JOHANN STRAUSS   Waltz from *Die Fledermaus*
IGOR STRAVINSKY   the finale from *The Firebird*
PYOTR ILYICH TCHAIKOVSKY   Panorama from *The Sleeping Beauty*
     Serenade for Strings
RALPH VAUGHAN WILLIAMS   Fantasia on a Theme of Thomas Tallis
     'Saraband for the Songs' from *Job*
     The Lark Ascending
     Rhosymedre
LOUIS VIERNE   The Finale to Symphony No. 1
     Larghetto from Symphonie No. 5
     Final (Symphonie No. 6)
HEITOR VILLA-LOBOS   Étude No. 11 in E minor
RICHARD WAGNER   Procession Music from *Lohengrin*
CHARLES-MARIE WIDOR   Toccata in F
     Toccata from Symphony V

OTHER:

The Last Post
The Reveillé
A miscellany of North Country Tunes: 'Blaydon Races'; 'On Ilkley
   Moor'; 'The Oak and the Ash'
'Port na bPúcai'
'Old Bush'
'Braes of Busby'
The South African College Schools song

The Contributors

MEMORIAL SERVICES

DAME PEGGY ASHCROFT DBE (1907–1991)
Westminster Abbey, 29 November 1991

Music: from productions of *The Wars of the Roses* and *All's Well That Ends Well*

THE SENTENCES

THE BIDDING

Hymn: 'Praise, my soul, the King of Heaven'

Reading: Dylan Thomas, 'And death shall have no dominion'

Sung: 'Gloria in excelsis Deo'

Reading: 1 Corinthians 13

Music: Heitor Villa-Lobos, Étude No 11 in E minor

ADDRESS

Reading: from William Shakespeare, *Cymbeline:* 'Fear no more the heat o' the sun'

Music: Wolfgang Amadeus Mozart, Piano Concerto in C, K467, Second Movement: Andante

ADDRESS

Sung: 'Laudate Dominum omnes gentes'; Wolfgang Amadeus Mozart, Psalm 117, 'O praise the Lord, all ye heathen'

PRAYERS

Sung: 'Bring us, O Lord God, at our last awakening'

Portraits: Juliet *by* Romeo from *Romeo and Juliet*; Katharina *by* Petruchio from *The Taming of the Shrew*; Queen Margaret *by* The Duke of York from *Henry VI Part III*; Beatrice *by* Benedick from *Much Ado About Nothing*; Desdemona *by* Othello from *Othello*; Cleopatra *by* Enobarbus from *Antony and Cleopatra*.

Hymn: 'Let all the world in every corner sing'

THE BLESSING

Readings: 'So, fare thee well' from William Shakespeare, *Antony and Cleopatra*; 'Our revels now are ended' from William Shakespeare, *The Tempest*

Music: J. S. Bach, Fantasia and Fugue in G minor BWV 542

⁂

SIR FREDERICK ASHTON OM, CH, CBE (1904–1988)

Westminster Abbey, 29 November 1988

Music: Constant Lambert, Prelude from *Horoscope*; Christoph Willibald Gluck, Dance of the Blessed Spirits from *Orfeo et Euridice*; J. S. Bach, arr. William Walton, 'Lord hear my longing' from *The Wise Virgins*; Pyotr Ilyich Tchaikovsky, Panorama from *The Sleeping Beauty*; Frédéric Chopin arr. Lanchbery, Andante spianato from *A Month in the Country*; Edward Elgar, 'Nimrod' from *Enigma* Variations; Wolfgang Amadeus Mozart, Andante from Piano Concerto K467

THE SENTENCES

THE BIDDING

Hymn: 'Praise to the Holiest in the height'

Reading: Ecclesiastes 3: 1–11

Sung: Psalm 121
'I will lift up mine eyes unto the hills'

Reading: from Marcel Proust, *À la Recherche du Temps Perdu*

THE ADDRESS

Music: Mozart, Piano Concerto in C major K 467, Second Movement: Andante

A TRIBUTE

PRAYERS

Hymn: 'Come down, O Love divine'

Prayer: 'Bring us, O Lord, at our last awakening'

THE BLESSING: 'Amen' by Orlando Gibbons

Music: J. S. Bach, Fantasia and Fugue in G minor BWV 542

※

JULIAN ROCHFORT BELFRAGE (1934–1994)

St James's Church, Piccadilly, 7 March 1995

Music: J. S. Bach, Prelude and Fugue in G; Georges Bizet, Duet from *The Pearl Fishers*

THE BIDDING

Hymn: 'Immortal, invisible, God only wise'

Readings: Canon Henry Scott Holland, 'Death Is Nothing At All'; Philip Larkin, 'At Grass'; 'Edward Thomas, 'Lights-Out'

Sung: Gabriel Fauré, 'Pie Jesu' (Requiem)

Readings: Revelation 21: 1–7; Hilaire Belloc, 'Lord Hippo'; a poem by Joyce Grenfell.

Sung: Leonard Bernstein, 'Tonight, Tonight' from *West Side Story*

Readings: A piece by Victor Hugo; Edward Lear, 'The Owl and the Pussycat'.

THE ADDRESS

Music: 'Port na bPúcai'; 'Old Bush' and 'Braes of Busby'

Readings: Max Beerbohm, 'Letter in Acknowledgement of wedding present' from *How shall I word it?*; Pearman, 'The Londonderry Air'.

Sung: 'Set Me as a Seal'

PRAYERS

Hymn: 'And did those feet in ancient time'

THE BLESSING

Sung: Frank Loesser, 'Sit down, you're rocking the boat' from *Guys and Dolls*

※

SIR JOHN BETJEMAN CBE (1906–1984)

Westminster Abbey, 29 June 1984

Music: Edward Elgar, Chanson De Matin; Albert Ketèlbey, In a Monastery Garden; Favourite School Songs; Edward Elgar; 'Nimrod' from *Enigma* Variations; Edward Elgar; Salut D'Amore; A Selection of Hymn Tunes

THE SENTENCES

THE BIDDING

Hymn: 'Immortal, invisible, God only wise'

Reading: Ecclesiasticus 44: 1–15

Sung: Psalm 150

Reading: Romans 8: 31–end

Sung: 'Thee, Lord, before the close of day'

THE ADDRESS

Hymn: 'When I survey the wondrous Cross'

PRAYERS

Readings: John Betjeman, 'Trebetherick'; 'South London Sketch, 1844'.

Hymn: 'Praise to the Holiest in the height'

Prayer: 'Bring us, O Lord, at our last awakening'

THE BLESSING

Music: J. S. Bach, Concerto in A minor, First Movement: Allegro; Charlie Parker, Pieces from *Banana Blush*: 'Indoor Games near Newbury', 'In the Public Gardens', 'The Cockney Amorist', 'A Shropshire Lad'.

RUPERT BIRLEY (1955–1986)

St James's Church, Piccadilly, 22 September 1986

THE BIDDING

Hymn: 'Dear Lord and Father of mankind'

Reading: John Donne, 'No man is an island, entire of itself'

Hymn: 'God Is'

ADDRESS

PRAYERS

THE BLESSING

Hymn: 'Abide with me; fast falls the eventide'

Anthem: 'The Lord's my Shepherd, I'll not want'

Sung: 'Up Where We Belong'

ROY CASTLE OBE

All Souls Church, Langham Place, 30 November 1994

PRAYER

TRIBUTE

Hymn: 'How sweet the name of Jesus sounds'

TRIBUTES

Hymn: 'When I survey the wondrous Cross'

BIBLE READING

Hymn: 'My song is love unknown'

PRAYERS

Hymn: 'Praise Him on the trumpet'

Reading: 'A Man Looks Back'

BIBLE READING

APPRECIATION

Hymn: 'How great Thou art'

BLESSING

❧

GROUP CAPTAIN LORD CHESHIRE OF WOODHALL
VC, OM, DSO, DFC (1917–1992)

Metropolitan Cathedral of The Most Precious Blood, Westminster,
25 September 1992

Music: George Frideric Handel, The Water Music

Hymn: 'All creatures of our God and King'

Music: Ralph Vaughan Williams, Kyrie from Mass in G minor

PRAYER

Reading: Wisdom 5: 16–17

Psalm: 'My soul is thirsting for the Lord: when shall I see him face to face?'

Reading: 1 Corinthians 13: 1–3

Sung: Alleluia (plainchant)

Reading: John 6: 51–58

HOMILY

PRAYERS

PREPARATION OF THE GIFTS

Music: Franz Schubert, Ave Maria

PRAYER OVER THE GIFTS

THE PREFACE

Music: Gabriel Fauré, Sanctus from Requiem

EUCHARISTIC PRAYER NO. 3

SIGN OF PEACE

Music: Ralph Vaughan Williams, Agnus Dei from Mass in G minor

Sung: Mozart, Ave Verum

Hymns: 'O Love that wilt not let me go'; 'Blest are the pure in heart'

PRAYERS

BLESSING

Sung: John Stainer, 'Amen'

Hymn: 'O valiant Hearts, who to your glory came'

Music: Frédéric Chopin, Funeral March from Sonata No. 1 Op 35; J. S. Bach, Jesu, Joy of Man's Desiring

---

DENHOLM ELLIOTT CBE (1922–1992)

St James's Church, Piccadilly, 19 January 1992

Music: George Frideric Handel, Music for the Royal Fireworks

BIDDING PRAYERS

Hymn: 'Praise my soul the King of heaven'

Reading: 'The Clarion'

ADDRESS

Sung: 'Oh for the wings of a dove'

Readings: Edward Lear, 'The Owl and the Pussycat'; 'The Rainbow Connection'; Lewis Carroll, 'Jabberwocky'; William Shakespeare, Sonnet 116; Poem to Dad and Serenity Prayer

Hymn: 'Jerusalem'

PRAYERS AND BLESSING

DAME MARGOT FONTEYN DE ARIAS DBE (1919–1991)

Westminster Abbey, 2 July 1991

Music: Edward Elgar, Salut d'amour; Maurice Ravel, Pavane pour une infante défunte; Gavin Gordon, 'Faithful Girl' from *The Rake's Progress*; Constant Lambert, 'Sarabande' from *Horoscope*; Franz Liszt, 'Marguerite and Armand' excerpt from Sonata in B minor; J. S. Bach arranged by William Walton, 'Lord hear my longing' from *The Wise Virgins*

THE SENTENCES

THE BIDDING

Hymn: 'O worship the King all glorious above'

Reading: 1 Corinthians 13

Sung: Psalm 23

ADDRESSES

Hymn: 'Father, hear the prayer we offer'

PRAYERS

Reading: William Chappell, 'Fonteyn – Impressions of a Ballerina'

Sung: Gabriel Fauré, 'In paradisum deducant Angeli' from *Requiem*

THE BLESSING

Music: Edward Elgar, Allegro maestoso from Sonata in G

DAME ELISABETH FRINK CH, DBE, RA (1930–1993)

St James's Church, Piccadilly, 21 September 1993

Hymn: 'Praise to the Lord, the Almighty, the King of creation'

BIDDING PRAYER

Reading: 1 Thessalonians 4: 13–18

Sung: Anton Bruckner, 'Kyrie' from Mass in E minor

Reading: Henry Scott Holland, 'Death is nothing at all'

Sung: Jauffre Rudel de Blaye, 'Lancan Li Jorn'

Reading: 'Let us be contented with what has happened to us'

Hymn: 'My song is love unknown'

A TRIBUTE

Music: J. S. Bach, Adagio and Fugue B W V 1001

THE ADDRESS

Sung: Johannes Brahms, 'How lovely are thy dwellings' *Requiem*

PRAYERS

Hymn: 'Now thank we all our God'

THE BLESSING

Music: Charles-Marie Widor, Toccata in F

IAN GOW TD, MP (1937–1990)

St Margaret's Church, Westminster Abbey, 22 October 1990

Music: J. S. Bach, 'Wachet auf, ruft uns die Stimme' BWV 645; Edward Elgar, 'Proficiscere amina Christiana' from *The Dream of Gerontius*; 'Nimrod' from *Enigma* Variations; J. S. Bach, 'Have mercy, Lord, on me' from St Matthew Passion BWV 244; 'In tears of grief' from St Matthew Passion

Sung: 'God be in my head'

THE BIDDING

Hymn: 'Immortal, invisible, God only wise'

Reading: St John 14: 1–14

Sung: 'Ave verum corpus, natum de Maria Virgine' '*Hail, true body, born of the blessed Virgin*'

PRAYERS

Reading: Joyce Grenfell, Excerpt from a letter, *Memorials, An Anthology of Poetry and Prose*

PRAYERS

Hymn: 'Holy, holy, holy! Lord God Almighty!'

THE ADDRESS

Sung: Nunc Dimittis, 'Lord, now lettest thou thy servant depart in peace'

Reading: Revelation 21: 1–7

Hymn: 'I vow to thee, my country, all earthly things above'

Music: 'The last post' and 'Reveille'

PRAYERS

THE BLESSING

Music: J. S. Bach, Toccata and Fugue in D minor BWV 565

The Right Honourable
THE LORD HAVERS OF ST EDMUNDSBURY PC (1923–1992)
The Temple Church, 8 June 1992

THE SENTENCES

Hymn: 'Dear Lord and Father of mankind'

Reading: Ecclesiastes 3: 1–15

Sung: 'God is gone up with a triumphant shout'

Hymn: 'All creatures of our God and King'

PRAYERS

THE ADDRESS

Hymn: 'And did those feet in ancient time'

THE BLESSING

Music: 'God be in my head, and in my understanding'

ELEANOR HIBBERT

St Peter's Church, Kensington Park Road, 6 March 1993

Music: Michael Praetorius, 'Es ist ein Ros' entsprungen'; Sigfrid Karg-Elert, 'Herzlich tut mich verlangen', 'O Gott, du frommer Gott'

PRAYER

Hymn: 'Praise, my soul, the King of heaven'

Reading: Psalm 121

Hymn: 'The King of love my Shepherd is'

Reading: John 14: 1–6

Sung: Thomas Tallis, 'If ye love me'

ADDRESS

Hymn: 'Abide with me; fast falls the eventide'

Reading: William Shakespeare, Sonnet No. 71

Sung: César Franck, 'Panis Angelicus'

ADDRESS

Hymn: 'The day thou gavest, Lord, is ended'

PRAYERS

Sung: Charles Villiers Stanford, 'Beati quorum via'

THE GRACE AND BLESSING

Hymn: 'Who would true valour see'

Music: J. S. Bach, 'In dir ist Freude'

JAMES HUNT (1947–1993)

St James's Church, Piccadilly, 29 September 1993

Music: J. S. Bach, St Anne Fugue in E flat; Mozart, Fantasia in F minor; Jeremiah Clarke, Trumpet Tune or 'The Prince of Denmark's March'

THE BIDDING

Hymn: 'Glorious things of thee are spoken'

Reading: Ecclesiastes 3

Hymn: 'Lord of all hopefulness, Lord of all joy'

Reading: Rudyard Kipling, 'If'

Sung: George Frideric Handel, 'The trumpet shall sound' from *Messiah*

Reading: Hilaire Belloc, 'Jim', from *Cautionary Tales for Children*

Hymn: 'Guide me, O Thou great Redeemer'

Reading: Psalm 84

Sung: George Frideric Handel, 'Zadok the Priest' from *George II's Coronation Anthem*

ADDRESS

PRAYERS

Hymn: 'Mine eyes have seen the glory of the coming of the Lord'

THE BLESSING

Music: Louis Vierne, The Finale to Symphony No.1; Sigfrid Karg-Elert, Marche Triomphale: Nun Danket Alle Gott

☙

JO

St James's Church, Piccadilly, 13 February 1995

THE BIDDING PRAYER

Hymn: 'Praise, my soul, the King of Heaven'

Reading: Lord Byron, 'She Walks In Beauty'

Sung: J. S. Bach/Gounod, 'Ave Maria'

Reading: Kahlil Gibran, 'Then Almitra spoke, saying, We would ask now of death'

Hymn: 'Dear Lord and Father of mankind'

ADDRESS

Sung: J. S. Bach, 'Have Mercy O Lord' from *St Matthew Passion*

PRAYERS

Hymn: 'Abide with me, fast falls the eventide'

Sung: Gabriel Fauré, 'Pie Jesu', 'In Paradisum' from *Requiem*

Reading: Walter Savage Landor, 'Death stands above me, whispering low'

BLESSING: God be in my head

Music: Antonín Dvořàk, Serenade for strings

OSBERT LANCASTER (1908–1986)

St Paul's Church, Covent Garden, 2 October 1986

Music: J. S. Bach, Prelude in B minor; Choral preludes

THE BIDDING

Hymn: 'O worship the King'

Reading: Proverbs 4: 4–13

Sung: Gioacchino Rossini, Aria from *Stabat Mater*

THE ADDRESS

Music: Mozart, String Quartet in C (K.465) First Movement: Adagio-Allegro

PRAYERS

Hymn: 'The spacious firmament on high'

THE BLESSING

Music: J. S. Bach, Fugue in F major

SIR ROBERT LUSTY (1909–1991)

St Paul's Church, Covent Garden, 2 October 1991

THE BIDDING

Hymn: 'God is working his purpose out as year succeeds to year'

Reading: Ecclesiastes 3: 1–8

ADDRESS

Sung: Psalm 121

ADDRESS

Sung: 'And I saw a new Heaven and a new Earth'

ADDRESS

Hymn: 'And did those feet in ancient time'

SIR KENNETH MacMILLAN (1929–1992)

Westminster Abbey, 17 February 1993

Music: Richard Rodgers, 'Waltz' from Carousel; Benjamin Britten, First Sea Interlude – Dawn; Maurice Ravel, Piano Concerto in G major (Adagio assai); Sergey Prokofiev, 'Balcony pas de deux' from *Romeo and Juliet*

THE SENTENCES

THE BIDDING

Hymn: 'Let all the world in every corner sing'

Reading: 1 Corinthians 13

Hymn: Psalm 23

Reading: C. Day Lewis, Verses from *Pegasus*

A TRIBUTE

Sung: Gustav Mahler, *The Song of the Earth*, Third song – About Youth

ADDRESSES

Sung: Benjamin Britten/Christopher Smart, 'Rejoice in God, O ye Tongues; give the glory to the Lord and the Lamb' from *Jubilate Agno*

PRAYERS

Hymn: 'O praise ye the Lord! praise him in the height'

Prayer: 'Bring us, O Lord God, at our last awakening'

THE BLESSING

Sung: Gabriel Fauré, 'Pie Jesu Domine' from *Requiem*

Music: Louis Vierne, Final (Symphonie No. 6)

❧

BOBBY MOORE OBE (1941–1993)

Westminster Abbey, 28 June 1993

Music: J. S. Bach, Toccata and Fugue in D minor BWV 538; Tomaso Giovanni Albinoni, Adagio in G minor; Johann Pachelbel, Canon in D

THE SENTENCES

THE BIDDING

Hymn: 'He who would valiant be'

Reading: Ecclesiastes 3: 1–11

Reading: from Kahlil Gibran, *The Prophet*: 'You would know the secret of death'

Hymn: 'The Lord's my shepherd, I'll not want'

ADDRESS

Sung: 'O for the wings of a dove!'

PRAYERS

Hymn: 'Abide with me; fast falls the eventide'

Reading: 1 Corinthians 13

ADDRESS

Hymn: 'And did those feet in ancient time'

THE BLESSING

Sung: 'God save our gracious Queen'

Music: Edward Elgar, Triumphal March from *Caractacus*

FOR THOSE WHO DIED
IN THE MOORGATE TRAIN DISASTER
28 February 1975

St Paul's Cathedral

Hymn: 'The King of love my Shepherd is'

Reading: Romans 8: 31–39

Sung: George Frideric Handel, 'I know that my redeemer liveth'

PRAYERS

Hymn: 'Jesu, Lover of my soul'

THE ADDRESS

Hymn: 'Jesus lives! thy terrors now'

THE BLESSING

Admiral of the Fleet
THE EARL MOUNTBATTEN OF BURMA
KG, PC, GCB, OM, GCSI, GCIE, GCVO, DSO, FRS (1900–1979)
DOREEN, LADY BRABOURNE CI, D.ST.J. (1896–1979)
THE HON. NICHOLAS KNATCHBULL (1964–1979)

St Paul's Cathedral, 20 December 1979

Hymn: 'Mine eyes have seen the glory of the coming of the Lord'

Reading: Romans 8: 35–38

Sung: Psalm 46

Reading: Revelation 21: 1–7

Sung: Felix Mendelssohn, 'I waited for the Lord, He inclined unto me,

He heard my complaint. O blessed are they that hope and trust in the Lord.' from the *Hymn of Praise*

THE ADDRESS

Hymn: 'Eternal Father, strong to save'

PRAYERS

Hymn: 'He who would valiant be'

Sung: 'God be in my head, and in my understanding'

PRAYERS

THE BLESSING

Sung: The National Anthem

⁂

NICOLETTE

St James's Church, Piccadilly, 22 November 1993

Sung: Psalm 119

THE BIDDING PRAYER

Hymn: 'The Lord's my Shepherd, I'll not want'

Reading: From T. S. Eliot, 'Ash Wednesday'

ADDRESS

Sung: Gabriel Fauré, 'Pie Jesu', 'Libera Me' and 'In Paradisum' from *Requiem*

PRAYERS

Sung: J. S. Bach/Gounod, 'Ave Maria'

Reading

Hymn: 'Dear Lord and Father of mankind'

Hymn: 'Abide with me; fast falls the eventide'

[229]

PRAYER

BLESSING

Music: Mozart, Divertimento K136

❧

The Right Reverend and Right Honourable
THE LORD RAMSEY OF CANTERBURY,
Archbishop of Canterbury 1961–1974

Westminster Abbey, 27 June 1988

Music: Basil Harwood, Dithyramb; Felix Mendelssohn, Sonata No. 4 in B flat; Henry Smart, Andante No. 1 in A; Dietrich Buxtehude, 'Komm heiliger Geist'

The Introit: William Byrd, 'Sacerdotes Domini incensum et panes offerunt Deo'. *'The priests of the Lord offer incense and bread to God'*

THE BIDDING

Hymn: 'Bright the vision that delighted'

Readings: from some of Bishop Michael Ramsey's books and sermons

Sung: 'Bless the Lord the God of our fathers'

Readings: St Mark 9: 2–8; Part of 2 Corinthians 3 and 4

Sung: 'Faire is the heaven where happy soules have place'

THE ADDRESS

Hymn: 'O Thou who camest from above'

THE PRAYERS

Hymn: 'Light's abode, celestial Salem'

THE BLESSING

Music: J. S. Bach, Prelude in E minor, BWV 548

❧

BRIAN REDHEAD (1929–1994)

St Paul's Cathedral, 23 March 1994

Music: J. S. Bach, Fantasia in G; A miscellany of North Country Tunes ('Blaydon Races'; 'On Ilkley Moor'; 'The Oak and the Ash'); John Stanley, Trumpet Tune; Flor Peeters, Aria; Alan Hovhaness, Prayer of St Gregory; Henry Purcell, Voluntary on the Old 100th; Joseph Wilcox Jenkins, Arioso

Reading: Henry Scott Holland, from the sermon *The King of Terrors*

Hymn: 'Now thank we all our God'

THE BIDDING

Sung: 'Come you not from Newcastle'

Reading: Romans 8: 14–25

Music: Johannes Brahms, Adagio, from Clarinet quintet in B minor, op. 115

Reading: from Frances Gumley and Brian Redhead, *The Christian Centuries*: 'The Sibyl of the Rhine' (Hildegard of Bingen)

Music: Frédéric Chopin, Largo, from Sonata in G minor, op. 65

Readings: from Brian Redhead, *The Inspiration of Landscape*: 'Northumberland', 'A Love of the Lakes', 'The National Parks: The Peak'.

Sung: 'Bring us, O Lord God, at our last awakening'

THE ADDRESS

Hymn: 'Breathe on me, Breath of God'

THE PRAYERS

Sung: 'I know that my redeemer liveth'

THE BLESSING

Music: Benny Goodman, 'Body and Soul'; J. S. Bach, Passacaglia and Fugue in C minor, BWV 582.

JEAN ROOK (1931–1991)

St Bride's Church, Fleet Street, 22 October 1991

Sung: Howard Blake, 'Walking in the Air' from *The Snowman*

BIDDING PRAYER

Hymn: 'The day thou gavest, Lord, is ended'

Reading: William Shakespeare, 'I pray thee, bear my former answer back' from *Henry V*, Act IV Scene III

Sung: Ennio Morricone, *The Mission*

ADDRESS

Hymn: 'Who would true valour see'

Readings: Jean Rook, 'Epitaph for Victor' from her *Daily Express* column; Christina Georgina Rossetti, 'Song' ('When I am dead, my dearest'); American Indian, 'Do Not Be Afraid'

Sung: 'Amazing Grace'

Reading: Ecclesiastes 3: 1–8

Sung: Thomas Tallis, 'If Ye Love Me'

ADDRESS

Music: Ralph Vaughan Williams, Fantasia on a Theme by Thomas Tallis

PRAYERS

Hymn: 'And did those feet in ancient time'

THE BLESSING

FRANKLIN DELANO ROOSEVELT (1882–1945)

St Paul's Cathedral, 17 April 1945

THE SENTENCES

Sung: 'Thou wilt keep him in perfect peace, whose mind is stayed on thee'

Sung: Psalm 23

Reading: Revelation 7: 9–17

Hymn: 'Fight the good fight with all thy might'

PRAYERS

THE GRACE

Hymn: 'The Battle Hymn of the Republic'

Sung: 'I heard a voice from heaven, saying unto me, Write, from henceforth blessed are the dead which die in the Lord; even so saith the Spirit; for they rest from their labours'

THE BLESSING

Music: 'The Last Post'; 'The Reveillé'; 'The Star-Spangled Banner'; The National Anthem

VISCOUNTESS ROTHERMERE (1929–1992)

St Bride's Church, Fleet Street, 1 October 1992

Music: Franz Schubert, String quartet in G major; Wolfgang Amadeus Mozart, String quartet K 156 in G major; Frank Bridge, Three idylls for string quartet

Sung: William McKie, 'We wait for thy loving kindness'

THE BIDDING

Hymn: Psalm 23

Reading: Psalm 142

Sung: Andrew Lloyd Webber, 'Pie Jesu' from *Requiem*

Hymn: 'Lead us, heavenly father, lead us'

Reading: from Kahlil Gibran, *The Prophet*: 'Then Almitra spoke, saying, We would ask now of Death'

Hymn: 'And did those feet in ancient time'

ADDRESS

PRAYERS

Sung: Sergey Rachmaninov, 'Vaskres iz groba'

BLESSING

Sung: John Stainer, Sevenfold Amen

Sung: Jo Collins, 'I'm in love with the world'

Music: John Addison, 'Reach for the Sky'; Ebb and Kander, 'New York, New York'

Reading: Jonathan, 'Farewell': 'It is with hearts of sorrow and thoughts of joy'

TESSA SAYLE (1932–1993)

St James's Church, Piccadilly, 30 September 1993

Music: Mozart, Fantasia in F minor and major

THE BIDDING PRAYER

Reading: Carol Ann Duffy, 'M–M–Memory'

Hymn: 'Praise, my soul, the King of heaven'

TRIBUTE

Sung: Johannes Brahms, 'How lovely are thy dwellings' from *Requiem*

TRIBUTE

Sung: Mozart, Kyrie from the Mass in C minor, K427

Reading: from Marcel Proust, *À la Recherche du Temps Perdu*

PRAYERS

Hymn: 'And did those feet in ancient time'

THE BLESSING

Music: Charles-Marie Widor, Toccata in F

❧

SIR PETER SCOTT CH, CBE, DSC, FRS (1909–1989)

St Paul's Cathedral, 20 November 1989

Reading: Henry Scott Holland, 'Death is nothing at all'

Music: J. S. Bach, Prelude and Fugue in G, BWV 541; George Frideric Handel, Suite from *The Water Music*; Gustav Mahler, Adagietto from Symphony No. 5; Franz Joseph Haydn, St Anthony Chorale; Felix Mendelssohn, Sonata No. 3 in A (First Movement)

Hymn: 'Praise my soul, the King of heaven'

THE BIDDING

Sung: Edgar Bainton, 'And I saw a new heaven and a new earth'

Reading: Psalm 104: 1–12

Sung: Psalm 121

Reading: Romans 8: 18–25

Hymn: 'Let all the world in every corner sing'

THE ADDRESS

Hymn: 'All creatures of our God and King'

THE PRAYERS

Hymn: 'Lord of beauty, thine the splendour'

Reading: Peter Scott, 'Who's God'

THE BLESSING

Sung: The National Anthem

❧

Edward Arthur Alexander,
THE RIGHT HONOURABLE LORD SHACKLETON
KG, AC, OBE, FRS (1911–1994)

Westminster Abbey, 25 January 1995

Music: Gustav Holst, Movements from Military Suite; Louis Vierne, Larghetto from Symphonie No. 5

Sung: Felix Mendelssohn, 'Lift thine eyes to the mountains, whence cometh help'

Hymn: 'Immortal, invisible, God only wise'

THE BIDDING

Reading: Wisdom 7: 15 – 8: 1

Sung: Psalm 104: 24–end

Reading: Philippians 4: 4–9

Hymn: 'Eternal Father, strong to save'

Readings: Hilaire Belloc, 'I shall go without companions'; John Donne, 'They shall awake as Jacob did, and say as Jacob said, Surely the Lord is in this place'

Sung: Franz Joseph Haydn, 'Achieved is the glorious work' from *The Creation*

THE ADDRESS

THE PRAYERS

Hymn: 'For all the Saints who from their labours rest'

THE BLESSING

Sung: Samuel Sebastian Wesley, 'Lead me, Lord, lead me in thy righteousness'

Music: Wolfgang Amadeus Mozart, Fantasia in F minor, K 608

THE RIGHT HONOURABLE JOHN SMITH qc, mp

Westminster Abbey, 14 July 1994

Music: Léon Boëllmann, Suite Gothique; Edward Elgar, 'Nimrod' (*Enigma* Variations); Malcolm Arnold, Siciliano (Suite for Brass)

Sung: Ralph Vaughan Williams, 'O taste and see how gracious the Lord is: blest is the man that trusteth in him'

Hymn: 'God is Love: let heav'n adore him'

THE BIDDING

Reading: Part of Isaiah 61

Sung: Psalm 15

Reading: Philippians 2: 1–11

Hymn: 'O Day of God, draw nigh'

THE ADDRESS

Sung: John Bunyan/Ralph Vaughan Williams, 'After this it was noised abroad that Mr Valiant-for-Truth was taken with a summons'

Reading: Gerard Manley Hopkins, 'Inversnaid'

THE PRAYERS

Sung: Iona Community, 'Watch, watch and pray, Jesus will keep to his word'

Hymn: 'Judge eternal, throned in splendour'

THE BLESSING

Sung: St Patrick/Charles Villiers Stanford, 'Christ be with me, Christ within me'

Music: J. S. Bach, Prelude in C minor, BWV 546; Richard Wagner, Procession Music, *Lohengrin*

MICHAEL SOMES CBE (1917–1994)

The Queen's Chapel of the Savoy, 9 February 1995

Music: Constant Lambert, 'Horoscope'; Glazunov, 'Birthday Offering'

Sung: National Anthem

THE BIDDING

Hymn: 'Immortal, invisible, God only wise'

THE SENTENCES

Sung: J. S. Bach, 'Be near me, Lord, when dying', from *St Matthew Passion*

Readings: Bishop Brent, 'The Ship'; 'Inspiration' from *Red Cloud Speaks*

Hymn: 'Come down, O Love divine'

A TRIBUTE

Music: Ralph Vaughan Williams, 'Saraband for the Son' from *Job*

A TRIBUTE

THE PRAYERS

THE COMMENDATION

Hymn: 'The day Thou gavest, Lord, is ended'

THE BLESSING

Sung: Nunc Dimittis; 'Lord, now lettest thou thy servant depart in peace'

Music: Igor Stravinsky, The finale from *The Firebird*

EDWARD JOHN, EIGHTH EARL SPENCER (1924–1992)

St Margaret's Church, Westminster Abbey, 19 May 1992

Music: César Franck, 'Pastorale'; J. S. Bach, 'Jesu, joy of man's desiring'; Edward Elgar, 'Nimrod' from *Enigma* Variations

Sung: 'God be in my head, and in my understanding'

THE BIDDING

Hymn: 'Immortal, invisible, God only wise'

Reading: Ecclesiastes 3: 1–14

Sung: Nunc Dimittis, 'Lord, now lettest thou thy servant depart in peace'

PRAYER

Music: Jean-Baptiste Loeillet, Gigue-Vivace, from Sonata in B flat for Trumpet and Organ

Hymn: 'I vow to thee, my country, all earthly things above'

THE ADDRESS

Sung: Gabriel Fauré, Sanctus, from *Requiem*

THE PRAYERS

Hymn: 'Thine be the glory, risen, conquering Son'

THE FINAL PRAYER

THE BLESSING

Sung: Orlando Gibbons, Three-fold Amen

Music: Charles-Marie Widor, Toccata from Symphony V

BILL TRAVERS (1922–1994)

St James's Church, Piccadilly, 28 June 1994

Music: Tomaso Giovanni Albinoni, Adagio

BIDDING PRAYER AND WELCOME

Hymn: 'Lord, bring the day to pass'

Readings: Arthur William Edgar O'Shaughnessey, 'Ode'; Emily Brontë, 'Often rebuked, yet always back returning'

Music: Ralph Vaughan Williams, 'The Lark ascending'

Readings: Virginia McKenna, 'Compassionate Crusader – For Bill'; Anne Morrow Lindbergh, 'Testament'; Ecclesiastes 3

Sung: Betty Botley/Frank Cordell, 'Ring of Bright Water'

Readings: from Kahlil Gibran, *The Prophet*: 'For what is it to die'; Francis Nnaggenda, 'The dead are not under the earth'

TRIBUTE

Reading: Elizabeth Jennings, 'More than an Elegy'

Music: Gustav Mahler, Symphony No. 5

Sung: 'God be in my head'

Hymn: 'All creatures of our God and King'

THE LORD'S PRAYER

THE BLESSING

Music: Tomaso Giovanni Albinoni, Adagio

DAME EVA TURNER DBE (1892–1990)

Westminster Abbey, 5 February 1991

Music: Mozart, Movements from Serenade No 10 in B flat major

THE SENTENCES

THE BIDDING

Hymn: 'The Lord's my shepherd, I'll not want'

Reading: 'Letter from Mozart to his dying father', 4 April 1787

Music: Giacomo Puccini, 'Chrysanthemums'

Reading: 1 Corinthians 15: 20–26, 35–38, 42–45, 53–58

Hymn: 'Fight the good fight with all thy might'

THE ADDRESS

Sung: Richard Wagner, 'Elisabeth's greeting' from *Tannhäuser*; Pietro Mascagni, 'Easter Hymn' from *Cavalleria Rusticana*; Giuseppe Verdi, 'Ingemisco' from *Requiem*; 'Va pensiero' from *Nabucco*.

PRAYERS

Sung: Giacomo Puccini, 'In questa reggia' from *Turandot*

Hymn: 'And did those feet in ancient time'

Prayer: 'Bring us, O Lord, at our last awakening'

THE BLESSING

Sung: Charles Villiers Stanford, 'Justorum animae in manu Dei sunt' *The souls of the righteous are in the hand of God*

Music: Edward Elgar, Sonata in G (First Movement)

SIR HUW WHELDON OBE, MC (1916–1986)

Westminster Abbey, 7 May 1986

Music: J. S. Bach, Fantasia in G major; Edward Elgar, Introduction and Allegro for Strings

THE SENTENCES

THE BIDDING

Hymn: 'Come down, O love divine'

Reading: Proverbs 3: 1–12

Sung: Henry Purcell, 'Dido's Lament' from *Dido and Aeneas*

Reading: St John 1: 1–18

Sung: Francis Poulenc, from Mass in G, Agnus Dei

TRIBUTES

Hymn: 'All people that on earth do dwell'

PRAYERS

Sung: George Frideric Handel, 'Zadok the priest'

PRAYER

THE BLESSING

Hymn: 'Immortal, invisible, God only wise'

Music: Marcel Dupré, Prelude and Fugue in B major

OTHER CONTRIBUTIONS

BRIAN ALDISS

Since I shall be moving towards the seventy mark when this volume appears, I approach the task of arranging my memorial service with some relish, appreciating that it may soon be of practical use.

To open: it has to be music, as grieving hordes shuffle into their seats. Sir Thomas Browne says, 'Happy are they that go to bed with grand music'. Mine would not be too grand. I would link my affection for Borodin with a love of travel and distance – and by this time I would be far enough away myself – and choose *The Steppes of Central Asia* by A. Borodin.

Then, in remembrance of Christian days, a hymn, the great hymn by Walter Chalmers Smith, described in the DNB as 'poet and preacher': 'Immortal, invisible, God only wise'. This hymn is full of thoughts about light (very suitable, considering that we all supposedly go into the world of light after snuffing it), culminating in that nice teaser, ''Tis only the splendour of light hideth Thee'.

The celebrants, having been reduced to a proper seriousness, will now hear a prose passage from Thomas Browne, physician of Norwich. Most appropriate will be passages from 'A Letter To a Friend Upon Occasion of Death of his Intimate Friend':

> Death hath not only particular Stars in Heaven, but malevolent Places on earth, which single out our Infirmities, and strike at our weaker Parts

And so on, grandly read . . .

By this time, a good laugh will be needed. A choice of drinks will circulate: a malt whisky such as Glenfiddich, grappa, a heavy red wine from Bulgaria, and San Pellegrino water (all with key associations) . . .

While the drinks circulate, we have a reading from *Lucky Jim* by Kingsley Amis. Chapter Six, where Dixon wakes to find 'a small creature of the night' has used his mouth first as a latrine, 'and then as its mausoleum'. And the trouble with the bedclothes.

Just to remind the celebrants that I also had aspirations towards comedy, Ken Campbell and Petronilla Whitfield, my old actor friends, with my partner, Frank Hatherley, producing as usual, will perform 'Bill Carter Takes Over' – my piece where God, proving a little counter-productive in some departments, is superseded by the eponymous Carter.

Cheerfulness having broken in, let's go with 'The Waiter and the Porter and the Upstairs Maid'. This is one of Johnny Mercer's brightest songs. He sings it with Bing Crosby and Mary Martin. It's about having fun. Another firm favourite is about not having fun; I identify strongly with 'Old Rivers', written by Cliff Crofford and sung or indited by the good old Western actor, Walter Brennan.

The celebrants now rise to deliver spontaneous tributes to my goodness and genius. This should not take more than a couple of minutes. Then whoever has drawn the short straw reads my poem – intended as consolation to the next generation –

The Path
O Lord, in whom I've sought to disbelieve,
    Look upon me.
Fortify an atheist's lack of faith.
    Look upon me.

That doesn't take long. Nevertheless, the congregation is glancing at its collective watches, so into *The Time Machine* by H.G. Wells, Chapter 14.

For everyone in his or her turn, death means the end of time. This sense finds memorable expression in Wells's story, when the Time Traveller reaches the end of our world, centuries hence:

> The darkness grew apace; a cold wind began to grow in freshening gusts from the east, and the showering white flakes in the air increased in number. From the edge of the sea came a ripple and whisper. Beyond these lifeless sounds the world was silent. Silent? It would be hard to convey the stillness of it. All the sounds of man, the bleatings of sheep, the cries of birds, the hum of insects, the stir that makes the background of our lives – all that was over . . .
>
> A horror of this great darkness came on me . . .

Thoroughly chastened, the celebrants snatch at what drink is left, swallow a last canapé, and depart to the strains of 'Brigg Fair' by Frederick Delius – that melancholy piece of jubilation.

(In the pub afterwards, the entertainment is improvised.)

DR MARY ARCHER

I would like to suggest the inclusion of this prayer, which I incorporated in my late Uncle Stanley's funeral service: 'Bring us, O Lord God, at our last awakening into the house and gate of heaven' by John Donne.

RICHARD BAKER

Music: Notturno for piano Trio in E Flat D 897 by Franz Schubert; the Evening Hymn and Sunset.

Readings: William Shakespeare, *The Tempest*, Act IV, Scene 1; T.S. Eliot, *Four Quartets*, 'We shall not cease from exploration' from 'Little Gidding'; William Shakespeare, from *Cymbeline*, 'Fear no more the heat o' th' Sun'; William Penn, 'They that love beyond the world cannot be separated by it.'

JOHN BIFFEN

To be held at
The Church of St Michael The Archangel
Llanyblodwel, Shropshire

Word: O be joyful in the Lord, all ye lands; serve the Lord with gladness and come before his presence with a song.

Hymn: 'Dear Lord and Father of mankind'

Confession: 'Let us confess to God the sins and shortcomings of the world'

Hymn: 'There is a green hill far away'

Reading: Hebrews 11

Hymn: 'Abide with me; fast falls the eventide'

Reading: 1 Corinthians 13: 1–10; 14: 11–13

Hymn: 'Lord of all hopefulness, Lord of all joy'

Sung: Franz Schubert, Ave Maria

Reading: 'Rabbi Ben Ezra', Verses I and II

Hymn: 'Guide me, O Thou Great Redeemer'

Reading: Rt Hon J. Enoch Powell, St George's Day Address, 22 April 1964

Sung: The National Anthem

Sung: 'The International' (Arise! ye starvelings from your slumbers)

CANON GEOFFREY BROWN

Music: Dietrich Buxtehude, 'Ach Herr, mich armen Sünder'

Hymn: Jan Struther, 'Lord of all hopefulness'

Reading: Ephesians 1:1–14

Sung: Psalm 121

Reading: From Kahlil Gibran, *The Prophet*

Sung: John Ireland, 'Greater love hath no man'

Reading: From Albert Schweitzer, *Memoirs from Childhood and Youth*

Music: Gregorio Allegri, Miserere

Reading: George Herbert, 'Love bade me welcome'

Music: Orlando Gibbons, Agnus Dei

Hymn: 'Guide me O Thou Great Redeemer'

Music: Ralph Vaughan Williams, Rhosymedre

MICHAEL DENISON

from his address for Dick Rawlinson:

Reading: for Dick the lover of his country and its peerless countryside, an Envoi from his old friend and mentor, Rudyard Kipling: 'Take of English earth as much'

KENT DURR

Hymn: 'He who would valiant be'

Reading: Ephesians 6:10–18

Sung: Felix Mendelssohn, 'O for the wings of a dove' from *Hear my Prayer*

Reading: Pope John XXIII from 'Journal of a Soul'

Hymn: 'I vow to thee, my country, all earthly things above'

ADDRESS

PRAYERS

Hymn: 'For all the saints who from their labours rest'

THE BLESSING

Sung: 'The Battle Hymn of the Republic'

Music: The South African College Schools song

DAVID FRENCH

Hymns: 'Ye holy angels bright'; 'God is working his purpose out'; 'O worship the Lord in the beauty of holiness'.

Readings: Rudyard Kipling, 'The Long Trail'; Teilhard de Chardin's

Hymn of the Universe, Pensée Number 20, Humanity in Progress; T.S. Eliot, Chorus Number 10 from *The Rock*.

Music: Percy Grainger, Harvest Hymn; Rutter, 'The Lord Bless You and Keep You'; Franz Joseph Haydn, 'The Heavens are Telling the Glory of God' from *The Creation*; Michael Tippett, 'Deep River' from *A Child of our Time*.

Prayers: 'If I should die and leave you here awhile'; Sir Francis Drake, 'See that ye hold fast the heritage we leave you, yea and teach your children its value, that never in the coming centuries their hearts may fail them, or their hands grow weak'; Committal Prayer from the Funeral Service; 'Go forth upon thy journey from this world, Oh Christian soul'.

❧

PETER HALL

Reading: From Plato, *The Last Days of Socrates*, 'I suspect that this thing that has happened to me is a blessing, and we are quite mistaken in supposing death to be an evil . . .'

❧

SUE LAWLEY

Henry Purcell's anthem 'Sound The Trumpet'

'A Valediction: Forbidding Mourning' by John Donne read by my husband, Hugh Williams

Hymn: 'Dear Lord and Father of mankind'

The adagio from Schubert's String Quintet in C major

The opening section from the comic novel *The Wimbledon Poisoner* read by the author, my brother-in-law, Nigel Williams

The duet for tenor and baritone 'Au fond du temple saint' from Act 1 of Bizet's *The Pearl Fishers*

'Naming of Parts' from Henry Reed's *Lessons of the War* read by my son, Tom Ashby

'I'm leaning on a lamp-post' (at the corner of the street . . .) from Noel Gay's *Me And My Gal* sung by my daughter, Harriet Ashby

Psalm 91: 'He that dwelleth in the secret place of the most High', read from the King James Bible

One of Mahler's Rückert Lieder 'Ich bin der Welt abhanden gekommen' ('I have lost touch with the world')

An extract from T.S. Eliot's *Four Quartets* beginning 'I said to my soul be still and wait without hope . . .' (from Part III of 'East Coker')

Hymn: 'Glorious things of thee are spoken'

Prayers

Rachmaninov's 'Rhapsody on a theme of Paganini'

⁂

MARTYN LEWIS

Reading: Henry Scott Holland, 'Death is nothing at all'

Hymns: 'Just as I am, without one plea'; 'He who would valiant be'; Jerusalem

⁂

JOANNA LUMLEY

Reading: Francis Nnaggenda, 'The dead are not under the earth'

(Joanna Lumley found this reading wonderfully comforting at a recent memorial service.)

⁂

JONATHAN MAGONET

(Meditations, Prayers and Translations are taken from *Forms of Prayer for Jewish Worship: Daily and Occasional Prayers*, Reform Synagogues of Great Britain)

Prayers: 'Let everyone cry out to God and lift our heart up to God'; 'Everything is given on pledge and a net is cast for all living'; 'Eternal God, source of all being and fountain of life, what can we say to You, for You see and know all thing.'

Sung: Jonathan Magonet (on tape) 'Bibo's Song'

ADDRESS

Sung: Jonathan Magonet (on tape) 'And it ain't no consolation'

And it ain't no consolation just to know I'm doing fine
Just to know I'm doing well it brings no comfort to my mind
For I know the game too well and it's an easy one to win
But whereabouts exactly does my life really begin.

I have heard with perfect hearing all the stories I can take
All the stories I can make to help the hours pass away
But the music is too moody and it hurts too much to smile
And what's the use pretending it can last more than a while.

It's a funny sort of feeling living on the edge of doubt
Living on the edge of shouting all the failure I can see
But what's the point of showing what is on the other side
Humility might only be another name for pride.

There's another sort of journey that is waiting very near
That is waiting very clearly for the moment to arrive
But will I then be ready when the final round is played
Is this the fear of heaven or am I just afraid?

Prayers: 'God of our strength, in our weakness help us'; 'El malei rachamim'/'God full of compassion whose presence is over us'

Sung: Jonathan Magonet (on tape) 'No obligation to buy'

No obligation to buy
No obligation to try
But if you still yearn
It's easy to learn
To fly.

Chorus:
Image when the ripples run
Shadow when there is no sun
And it's done.

Life in a children's game
Death is the pretty frame
So little time
And only a rhyme
To blame.
Chorus

Souls in the market place
Buy success or grace
But things that they sell
Are only the shell
Of a face.
Chorus

No obligation to buy
No obligation to try
But if you still yearn
It's easy to learn
To fly

Image when the ripples run
Shadow when there is no sun
And it's done.

Prayer: Kaddish (the mourner's prayer)

Sung: Jonathan Magonet (on tape) 'Cavalcade'.
   Serve him his supper when the singer comes to call
   Take off his weariness and hang it in the hall
   He cannot stay long and his needs are very small
   Chorus: And you may never see his like again
       So hang on, don't be afraid
       You can join the cavalcade.

It isn't nice to see the way the prophet eats
He tends to dribble and he's far too fond of sweets
But when it matters he's the one who never cheats.
Chorus

Don't scare the poet who is hiding underground
Though bombs are falling only he can hear the sound
If words can heal you better let him stay around
Chorus

The teacher's tenderness as strong as it is clear
Using his glasses you can see beyond your fear
And watch with wonder as he'll slowly disappear
Chorus

The grey-haired mother who likes her whisky neat
Without intending she's adopted half the street
Though she has nothing she will always make ends meet
Chorus

The clown is innocent, the clown is very nice
And just enough a clown to have to pay the price
He's strangely wise but always takes the wrong advice
Chorus

The scholar sits upon his unexpected throne
Giving a hint of the infinity he's known
Protected by a little whimsy of his own.
Chorus

The dancer waltzing through the nightmares of the past
Working in parables and dreams that have to last
Knowing the dangers when the music plays too fast.
Chorus

The cast assembled, the overture begins
Parading angels in their badly-fitting skins
Off-stage the invisible director slowly grins
And you may never see his like again
So hang on, don't be afraid
You can join the cavalcade.

SYBIL MARSHALL

I would like to be remembered by my family and friends in much the same way as they thought of me while I was alive – which will, I think, probably produce more fun than grief, more tears of laughter than of sorrow. As everyone will have different memories, in compiling the list below I have cast the net of my own memory wide so as to catch as many in common as possible. Love has been my guiding star, words my medium, and laughter, as Rupert Brooke said, 'The very garland on the head of friendship'. Remember me like that.

East Anglian Folk-song: 'The life of a man is the life of a leaf'

Poem: 'Gaudeamus Igitur' (Come, no more of grief and dying) by Margaret L. Woods

Hymn: 'Immortal, invisible, God only wise'

Readings:
(a) From Thomas Traherne's *Thanksgiving for the Body* (lines 85–127)
(b) Proverbs 3: 13–17

Music: Bach, Double Concerto for two Violins: Second Movement, Largo ma non tanto

Poem: 'Valediction forbidding Mourning' by John Donne

Music: Beethoven, Symphony No 6, The Pastoral: Third Movement, 'Peasants dancing'; Waltz sequence, played by Charlie Kunz, from *Focus on Charlie Kunz*

Reading: 'In which Piglet meets the Heffalump' by A.A. Milne

Music: 'Alleluia' from 'Exsultate jubilate' by Mozart. Sung by Dame Kiri te Kanawa

Poem: 'When the Moon's splendour shines in naked heaven' by Wilfrid Strabo, trans. Helen Waddell

Hymn: 'The King of love my shepherd is'

Celtic Benediction

YEHUDI MENUHIN

My choice for my memorial service: Waltz from Johann Strauss, *Die Fledermaus*:

> Glücklich ist wer vergisst was doch nicht zu ändern ist.
> *Happy he, who forswears that o'er which he hath no sway*

A most characteristic Austrian philosophy.

❧

REVEREND JANE MILLARD
Chaplain to People with HIV/AIDS

A service for remembering my Daddy

This is the programme of a service which a four-year-old child helped to compile and take for her, her family and her father's friends and colleagues as a memorial service for her Daddy. Four-year-olds are quite bossy!

1. Jane says hello and things.
2. I choose a big memorial candle and light it to start the service.
3. Jane remembers about Daddy being sick and dying, and tells the story of Daddy's life. A man from work and Uncle help.
4. Jane asks me if I can tell the story about when I made my Daddy cross, and after, another one when Daddy made me giggly.
5. Then we all get some crayons and paper and can draw something that we want to remember about Daddy. It can be good or bad, sad or happy. The grown-ups can do this too, or write.
6. We have some music while we do this.
7. Jane reads us the story about a loving father and talks to us about it. (St Luke Ch 15: 20–24)
8. We give our pictures to Jane and she tells us about love, memories and remembering real people, not only the good bits.
9. Outside there will be helium balloons for everyone. We can remember something about Daddy that we find hard to let go of, or sore to think about.

10. We all have to be quiet and still for a moment to think about this.
11. Then Jane says can we think of a hope to fly for the future as we watch the balloons fly.
12. Jane brings me and Auntie the memorial candle to blow out because Daddy's service has finished.
13. We go outside to remind ourselves that we can let go of things by letting go of the balloons, and to fly our hopes for the future.
14. Jane gives me the pictures we made in the service, tied up in pretty ribbon, for my memory box.
15. We say thank you for Daddy, and thank you to everyone for coming.
16. Then we go for juice and buns, but the grown-ups can get tea and things.

JAN PIENKOWSKI

Hymn: 'Let all mortal flesh keep silence'

ERIN PIZZEY

In Memoriam

As my life is one long party, I expect the following upon my demise:

The Savoy Hotel to reserve my usual River Room suite for the party.

Rosso di Montalcino 1990 arguably the best year of this century.

Food plays such a large part in my life that I will have provided the hotel with my own hand-made sausages, buristo, prosciutto and capricolo.

All lovers past and present to be included but no husbands.

The announcement in *The Times* to read:

> After a surfeit of sex and food Erin Pizzey passed away on her black satin sheets with a smile of satisfaction on her face. She

would like it to be known that she paid none of her debts, forgave none of her enemies and has taken no secrets to her grave.

Her secrets will be published on the day of her funeral in the *News of the World* for a disclosed sum of money of two million pounds.

Her autobiography will shatter what little peace the Great and the Good have managed to find upon hearing of her death.

Her son Amos Pizzey will sing his latest best-selling record with her friend Boy George. A purple passage from her latest book *Kisses* will be read to a hopefully blushing audience.

Red Ken along with Peter Tatchell (who took the children to the park for me from the Refuge, Chiswick Women's Aid) to lead the dancing.

Everybody to be reminded that Peter Pan said that dying is a great adventure. I shall be watching my party with great interest and no regrets. I shall continue to play havoc but now in God's great universe.

R.W.F. POOLE

This is the address that I wrote for the funeral of my little nephew, who died of a cot death.

ADDRESS

Little Michael has gone from us and we are grieving. It is meet and right that we should do so. But we are also here to celebrate Michael's short life and it was a cause for celebration – celebration for all the joy that he brought to all those who knew him.

There is another cause for joy as well. Michael's life may have been sadly short, but it was a life in which he knew nothing but love, laughter and happiness. Any tears he shed were those of any normal happy child. He will never know the pain, fear, uncertainty and black despair that come to all of us who live longer lives. Michael is now holding the hand of God and will know nothing but everlasting happiness. We should indeed be joyful for him.

Of course, those he has left behind feel pain and misery at losing him. But he is not lost – he has just gone through the door that we shall all have to go through one day. When we do, Michael and all our other loved ones will be waiting to greet us. How do I know this? I do not, but I believe it.

So let us keep the memory of Michael clear and dear in our hearts and look forward to the day when we shall see him again. Until then let us strive for happiness. Michael was such a happy child. He would want us to be happy too.

☙

ESTHER RANTZEN

Slow Movement from Brahms Double Concerto for violin and cello

Poem by John Donne, 'Song'

Dorothy Parker, 'One Perfect Rose'

Edith Piaf, 'Je ne regrette rien'

Opening of the first chapter of *Pride and Prejudice* by Jane Austen

Ella Fitzgerald, 'Life is just a bowl of cherries'

Corinthians 13

Gymnopediés by Satie

Readings individually chosen by Desmond, Emily, Rebecca and Joshua

Mozart's Piano Concerto in C, the slow movement 'The Elvira Madigan theme' by Amanda Thompson.

☙

CLAIRE RAYNER

My Gawd! Design my own memorial service! I can tell you in very short terms already what it will be. A jolly cremation with music, being all New Orleans Funeral Jazz – really good bouncing dolorous yet happy stuff of the sort I'm told you can hear in the streets there any time. My son Jay will know the sort I'd like! Afterwards, I'd want there to be a zonking great party with lots of food and drink for everyone so that they can swop stories about what a nice person I had been and the funny things I'd said. And then I'd want them all to go home and get on with life and just be glad I'd been around as long as I had and to hell with the fact that I no longer was.

P.S. Oh, and nothing religious at the cremation, of course; just someone who knew me and liked me, to say funny things and make people laugh.

❧

MISS READ (DORA SAINT)

Music: Tchaikovsky, Serenade for strings; Schumann, Piano Concerto in A minor

Hymns: 'Praise my soul the King of heaven'; 'Ye holy angels bright'; 'Sunset and evening star'.

Reading: Shakespeare, *Cymbeline*, 'Fear no more the heat o' the sun'

Prayer: Lord's Prayer: 'Our Father *which* art in heaven'

Music: Nunc Dimittis

❧

DOROTHY TUTIN: For my mother

Music: Handel, 'I know that my Redeemer liveth'; Mendelssohn, 'O, for the wings of a dove'

Hymn: 'Praise, my soul, the King of Heaven'

Reading: Henry Scott Holland, 'Death is nothing at all'

Sung: 'God be in my head'

Reading: Kahlil Gibran, *The Prophet*, 'For what is it to die'

Music: Nunc Dimittis, 'Lord now lettest thou in servant depart in peace'

PRAYERS

Music: 'Spread a little happiness'

❧

PAULINE WEBB

Hymn: 'O Thou who camest from above'

Prayers: 'O Lord, the first and the last, the beginning and the end'; 'Bring us, O Lord God, at our last awakening'

Readings: Psalm 139; Revelation 21: 1–7

Hymn: 'Love divine, all loves excelling'

Readings: Tagore, 'Farewell my Friends'

Sung: Bette Midler, 'The wind beneath my wings'

Readings: Anon, 'I have seen death too often to believe in death'; Pauline Webb, 'I don't believe in death'; Joyce Grenfell, 'If I should go before the rest of you'

Hymn: 'Thine be the glory, risen, conquering Son'

Reading: Sybil Thorndike, 'What a lovely party! And how much she must have enjoyed it! When's the next Memorial Service?'

⁂

ARNOLD WESKER

Reading: from *Love Letters On Blue Paper*

⁂

AUTHOR AND COMPOSER INDEX

TITLE INDEX

INDEX OF CONTRIBUTORS

INDEX OF FIRST LINES

ACKNOWLEDGEMENTS

For assistance in the preparation of this book, Michael Joseph Ltd are grateful to Canon John Oates and Robert Jones, Director of Music, of St Bride's, Fleet Street; the Reverend Donald Reeves of St James's, Piccadilly; the Very Reverend Eric Evans, Dean, and Jo Wisdom, Librarian, of St Paul's Cathedral; the Very Reverend David Elliott of St Paul's, Covent Garden; and the Reverend Canon Dr Donald Gray of St Margaret's, Westminster, and Westminster Abbey. The services of Franklin Roosevelt and those who died in the Moorgate Train Disaster are reproduced by permission of the Dean and Chapter of St Paul's Cathedral.

Every reasonable effort has been made to contact copyright owners for quoted material; the publishers will be happy to rectify any omissions in future editions. The publishers gratefully acknowledge the following for permission to reproduce copyright material:

Mrs Riechmann for 'How Shall I Word It' by Max Beerbohm; 'Tonight' by Leonard Bernstein, Stephen Sondheim, copyright © 1957 (renewed) Leonard Bernstein, Stephen Sondheim, Jalni Publications Inc., USA and Canadian publisher G. Schirmer Inc., worldwide print rights and publisher rest of the world. Campbell Connelly & Co. Ltd, 8/9 Frith St, London W1V 5TZ, international copyright secured, all rights reserved; 'I Shall Go Without Companions', 'Jim' and 'Lord Hippo' from *Complete Verse* by Hilaire Belloc, published by Jonathan Cape/Pimlico, reprinted by permission of the Peters Fraser & Dunlop Group Ltd; 'London Sketch' and 'Trebetherick' from *Collected Poems* by John Betjeman, published by John Murray (Publishers) Ltd; extracts from the Authorized Version of the Bible (The King James Bible), the rights in which are vested in the Crown, are reproduced by permission of the Crown's Patentee, Cambridge University Press; 'Lost Am I to the World'; English translation copyright © George Bird and Richard Stokes 1976 (*The Fischer-Dieskau Book of Lieder*, published by Victor Gollancz Ltd); 'Walking in the Air' by Howard Blake, copyright © 1962 by Highbridge Music Ltd, publishing rights administered by Faber Music Ltd, reprinted by permission; 'Life is Just a Bowl of Cherries' by Lew Brown and Ray Henderson, copyright © 1973 Chappell – Cc Inc, USA, reproduced by permission of International Music Publications Ltd; 'Old Rivers' by Cliff Crofford, copyright © 1962 Glo Mac Music-Metric Music Co., USA; Cinephonic Music Co. Ltd, 8/9 Frith St, London W1V 5TZ, international copyright secured, all rights reserved; 'M-M-Memory' by Carol Ann Duffy is taken from *The Other Country*, and published by Anvil Press Poetry in 1991; extracts from 'Choruses from "The Rock"' and 'Little Gidding' from *Collected Poems 1909–1962* by T.S. Eliot, published by Faber and Faber Ltd; 'Leaning on a Lamp Post' by Noel Gay, copyright © 1937 Richard Armitage Ltd/ Cineophonic Music Co. Ltd, 8/9 Frith St, London W1V 5TZ, internationl copyright secured, all rights reserved; Richard Scott Simon Limited for permission to reproduce an extract from *Memorials: an Anthology of Poetry and Prose* by Joyce Grenfell, published by Macmillan General Books; 'If I Should Go Before the Rest of You' from *Joyce by Herself and Her Friends*, published by Macmillan General Books; extract reproduced from *The Christian Centuries* by Francis Gumley and

Brian Redhead with the permission of BBC Worldwide Limited; the Hon. Jonathan Harmsworth for 'Farewell'; David Higham Associations for 'More than an Elegy' from *Collected Poems* by Elizabeth Jennings; the estate of Terence Kilmartin for translations from *Remembrance of Things Past* by Marcel Proust, published by Chatto and Windus Ltd; 'If', 'The Long Trail' and 'A Charm' by Rudyard Kipling reproduced by permission of A.P. Watt Ltd on behalf of The National Trust for Places of Historic Interest or Natural Beauty; 'At Grass' by Philip Larkin is reprinted from *The Less Deceived* by permission of the Marvell Press, England and Australia; 'The Waiter and the Porter and the Upstairs Maid' from 'The Birth of the Blues' by Johnny Mercer, copyright © 1941, renewed 1968, Famous Music Corporation, reprinted by permission, all rights reserved; extract from *Winnie the Pooh* by A. A. Milne, published by Methuen Children's Books (an imprint of Reed Books); Reverend Stephen Oliver, Rector of Leeds, for permission to reproduce prayer first broadcast on BBC Radio 4's *Daily Service;* 'One Perfect Rose' from *The Collected Dorothy Parker* by Dorothy Parker by permission of Gerald Duckworth and Co Ltd; extract from *Inspiration of Landscape: Artists in National Parks,* edited by Brian Redhead, published by Phaidon Press Ltd; translation of Pensée 20 from *Hymne de l'univers* by Pierre Teilhard de Chardin copyright © Editions du Seuil, 1961; 'And Death Shall Have No Dominion' from *The Poems* by Dylan Thomas, published by J.M. Dent; 'Deep River' from *A Child of Our Time* by Michael Tippett, reproduced by kind permission of Schott & Co Ltd; A.P. Watt Ltd on behalf of the Literary Executors of the Estate of H.G. Wells for an extract from *The Time Machine;* extract from *The Wimbledon Poisoner* by Nigel Williams, published by Faber and Faber Ltd; to her grandson, Major-General Henry Woods and her great-niece, Mrs Henry Woods, for permission to reproduce 'Gaudeamus Igitur' by Margaret L. Woods, the late nineteenth- and early twentieth-century poet and novelist, whose poetry is distinguished by a particular sensitivity for the natural world, and whose novels, some historical, delineate truly believable characters and plots.